Praise for Plan to Be Flexible

"Although I have homeschooled for several years now, I found *Plan to Be Flexible* to be full of practical advice gleaned from real-life experiences. It really is a study guide for learning to plan and organize your school days!" *–Brandy Ferrell of HalfAHundredAcreWood.com*

"Alicia wrote about things I had not even thought of before. When I first started reading the book, I felt like Alicia was in my living room talking to me as a friend. This book is a very easy read and has so much information. I especially liked the action plans at the end of each chapter. *Plan to Be Flexible* has given me so many new ideas and tips to try out."*–Rebecca of Our Life–Home and School blog*

"This book was invaluable for a beginning homeschooler like me. What an incredible resource for planning our future as a homeschool family!"*–Heidi, homeschool mom of three*

"In the first pages alone, *Plan to Be Flexible* spoke so clearly and loudly to my heart. My son and I do school right now with clenched fists and teeth. It is not inspiring or encouraging, and no one is really getting anything lovely out of it. But this book has given such a beautiful vision—a clarity as to what we must do as parents to truly cultivate a love of learning in our children (while still building relationships). This book has been a wonderful guide to walk us toward healing and wholeness."*–Jennifer King of WorthABowedHead.com*

"I found myself wanting to take a dip into this fun and creative world that Alicia describes throughout the book. I even had moments wishing that I was one of her kids in this home that doesn't live confined to a calendar or clock, but strives to make life the library of learning. Reading this felt like an afternoon of coffee with a close friend that you don't want to end."--*Caryn, homeschool mom of two*

"I'm very grateful for this book because it has given me a clear vision to recognize when learning is taking place amidst the chaos and messes of everyday life, and has given me the motivation to be willing to bravely recognize the opportunities for real and truthful learning (even if it involves messiness) and to embrace them with joy. Alicia invites us to envision a beautifully flexible and purposeful learning life." —*Maritza Antunez of HomeschoolingEphiphany.com*

"I thoroughly enjoyed *Plan to Be Flexible* and encourage others to read it. I liked her ideas and concepts so much that I am completely redoing my schedule for the year!"--*Janeen of SproutingTadpoles.com*

"Homeschooling families will appreciate Alicia's refreshingly simple approach to tackling organization and flexibility--two keys to a successful learning environment. Whether readers are new to homeschooling, or have years of experience, this book gives invaluable tips in how to organize your homeschool while maintaining enough flexibility for everyday life."–*Eryn, homeschool mom of four*

"*Plan to Be Flexible* gets down to the nitty gritty of figuring out what is working in your homeschooling process–and what is not. This book is very realistic as Alicia mentions many different challenges different families have when they homeschool and how they can keep making progress despite those challenges, and what to do when life gets in the way. If you are a homeschooling mom, you will want this book!"— *Tammy of CreativeKKids.com*

"*Plan to Be Flexible* is replete with first-hand, Christ-directed examples from her family's school days. Alicia's approach explores how to maintain the utmost confidence as academics, life skills, and spiritual character are instilled—no matter the season of life. I loved this book!"—*Kelli, homeschool mom of six*

"I so much appreciated Alicia's encouragement to look at all of life as a learning opportunity, and also to give yourself grace on the hard days." –*Joy of Artful Homemaking.com*

"There is a lot of good advice in this book. My favorite part is the assessment portion in the appendix of the book. What a great guide to help you get an idea of where you are at and where you need to go to achieve your goals!"—*Erin of AmundsenHouseofChaos.com*

"I found Alicia's style to be very personable, real, intelligent, and professional. She's been homeschooling long enough, and with enough kids, to have some great background to work from. She writes like a friend you can sit down and be real with, because you know she's being real with you." –*Jody of BecauseImMe.com*

PLAN TO BE

Designing A Homeschool Rhythm
and Curriculum Plan that Works for Your Family

by Alicia Michelle

Acknowledgments

To my friends and writing mentors who took the time to examine every page of this book: I am grateful for all your edits and recommendations! You encouraged me to share my personal experiences in the book, and *Plan to Be Flexible* is so much better for it. Thank you, thank you.

To those wonderful homeschool moms who continue to strengthen me on my journey: Your stories and advice are the God-given balm for those days when I am tired and doubting. Thank you for your inspiration and leadership.

To Annabelle Tague: thank you for your mad proofreading skills. You have a wonderfully bright future ahead in journalism!

To Cassie Lee: once again, your photos are extraordinary! Thank you for our fun afternoon of photos, pizza and pool play.

To Sharon Marta: you made my book look beautiful! You have given your time and talents over and over to me, and I am so thankful. May the Kingdom of God be blessed by your incredible flair for design.

To my four beautiful children who've given me lots to write about: How I treasure each of you and am thrilled to watch you grow! You are each extraordinary people and, as a result, I know your lives for God will be anything but ordinary. I will forever be cheering for you! I love you and am privileged to be called your mom.

To my precious TDK, my constant and my faithful: You have walked with me through every hill and valley of our homeschool journey. I'm so grateful for your listening ear, godly wisdom and servant heart. I could not live this life without you, my wonderful husband and confidante. I love you.

To the Lord Jesus who has not only created me in His image, but who has blessed me with an incredible life here on earth and an indescribably wonderful eternal life ahead: You birthed this book in me, and gave me every single word. Time and time again you proved your faithfulness by providing the examples, the stories and the wisdom. I am honored and exceedingly humbled to be used by you. My sincere prayer is that what's contained in these pages will change lives and bring you all the glory and honor for it.

To the Master Teacher who guides this student every day

Contents

Introduction

This book is for the planners out there: those homeschool moms who, like me, love the beauty of a well-ordered day.

It's also **for those women who are not planners by nature** but who long to be more organized.

But mostly, **this book is for those women (planners or non-planners) who have tried over and over to organize their homeschool days and have felt like an utter failure as they watched their well-laid plans fall to pieces.** Those moms who've spent hours on intricate lesson plans only to see a child say, "Do we have to do this...?" Moms who have woken up to a house full of runny-nosed, coughing children who need more of a mommy than a teacher that day. My guess is if you've been homeschooling for more than two minutes you can relate (and you can fill in your own situations).

This book was born out of my own tears and endless trial and error. I have tried many systems and schedules and have found myself completely frustrated that each new "miracle" method didn't work long-term.

My days were not organized, no matter how much I tried to make them that way. If I did find a method that worked, it seemed like it was too rigid. The kids quickly tired of a strict routine (and frankly, so did I). Alternatively, our planned schoolwork sometimes didn't fit perfectly in the time constraints we'd created, and therefore had to be added to the next day's work. Either way, we'd all end up frustrated and irritated at each other by the end of the day.

Was it the curriculum that wasn't working? Yes, I discovered that sometimes a fresh new curriculum helped. Did I need to change how I presented some of the information and introduce new teaching methods? I did that, and it helped a little too.

However, the biggest change came when I realized that my desire to have everything perfectly planned out was the true source of our frustration. I'd been holding on so tight to my need for a specific schedule that I'd fallen into the habit of letting anger, frustration and a "just get it done" attitude become a part of our days. Those incredibly frustrating days had become more the rule than the exception and homeschooling had become a burden.

I had to ask myself: **Was school really fun...for me or the kids?** Where was the exploration, the joy of learning? It wasn't happening when I felt like a drill sergeant instead of a servant-leader to my kids. I wanted us to have the freedom to explore a topic further and to let them express what they'd been learning in their own unique style; but how was that to happen within a schedule? And how could I make sure that what we were doing every day was in line with our original intentions for homeschooling?

With four kids to teach (plus my roles in running the home, loving my husband, maintaining family relationships, developing friendships with other women, serving at the church, running the blog, etc.) **I knew that organization was essential to survival, but I didn't want to sacrifice the joy of learning (and family relationships) for a rigid schedule.**

Was there a way to **combine good organization** (even several months or even a year in advance) **with free-flowing, student-directed learning**—all while still meeting our big-picture homeschooling goals—I wondered? I sure hoped so.

This is my journey of discovering that way of schooling: a way to satisfy both my type-A planner personality and my house full of curious, ever-evolving, sometimes-unpredictable students. **It is my explanation of how to put together an organized daily rhythm that accomplishes big-picture homeschooling goals and leaves room for real-life learning (and real-life).**

This is the book that I wish someone had written for me, especially when I was first starting out.

INTRODUCTION

It's not a 10-step method to a perfectly planned schedule (although we will talk about targeting goals through daily and weekly rhythms).

Nor is it a listing of the "correct" methods in which to school (however, I will share what works for us).

Instead, it's meant to **help you develop a plan that is organized yet flexible for your ever-changing family dynamics.**

This book is meant to **challenge some deep concepts about how you homeschool.** Concepts like "we are going to do whatever the curriculum tells us, whether we like it or not" that you may have developed to survive those first few years of teaching.

The book will also help you **consider your overall goals for educating your children** (this year and beyond) so that you can begin implementing these long-term goals into your everyday schooling. What goals have you set not only for where you want your children to be educationally, but socially and emotionally by the end of the next school year? This will give you guideposts—targets to shoot for—as you determine how to make the most of your time, and thus which elements of your days are non-negotiables.

Lastly, yes, **this book is a compilation of organizational tips** so that you can combine your unique goals and homeschool methods into a living and workable daily homeschool rhythm.

I've also compiled a list of posts ("Plan to Be Flexible: For Additional Insight") that give more information on the topics covered in each chapter. These posts are listed, by chapter, on the Vibrant Homeschooling website at http://bit.ly/1D3OvvQ .

In addition, the "Recommended Homeschooling Resources" page on the Vibrant Homeschooling blog (http://bit.ly/1yLeJ0P) contains a listing of some of our family's favorite homeschooling tools and resources, and links to my Pinterest boards.

I am excited to walk on this journey with you as we discover **what will not only bring order and peace to our days, but what will make our teaching time**—these precious moments we've been given with our kids!— **much more purposeful and productive.**

PART 1:

Establish and Refine Goals

CHAPTER 1:

The Finish Line as Daily Guide

The doorbell rang promptly at 8:00 a.m. "Of course she's right on time," I grumbled to myself, gently sliding the now-dozing baby off my chest and onto the bed next to me.

I rubbed my eyes after the long night with my sleepless newborn and then began the painful process of slowly easing myself off my bed, the week-old Cesarean stitches still angry and sore.

"Miss Marli's here! Miss Marli's here!" the children chorused through the house, all running in merriment to the front door.

"Mom, can we open the door?" my oldest excitedly called up the stairs to me.

"Sure," I managed weakly, glad to not have to hustle myself down the stairs to open it myself.

The door creaked open and I heard a familiar, "Hey guys!"

Marli, an eighteen-year-old homeschooler from our church, had known almost all of my kids since they were infants. As our pastor's daughter

1

and the eldest of six kids, we trusted her implicitly and were thrilled when she'd agreed to help out a few days a week after the birth of our fourth baby.

She embraced each of my kids with a big hug and a few excited greetings. Then suddenly her voice got a little quieter. "Is your momma upstairs with the new baby?"

The kids nodded, grabbed her hand and beckoned her to, "Come see! Come see!"

They bounded up the stairs toward my closed bedroom door, Marli in tow. My daughter ran down the hall and loudly grabbed the door handle, eager to show her friend the tiny new treasure that lay inside.

"Oh! Shhh..." Marli said gently. "Better not open the door. The baby might be sleeping."

By this time I'd hobbled to the door and opened it myself. "Good morning, Marli," I whispered quietly, managing a smile.

"Good morning, Mrs. Kazsuk!" she said in a cheery whisper. She glanced at the bed where my nine-pound bundle lay, swaddled as snugly as a Christmas present. She also noticed my bloodshot eyes and how I looked...well, probably not how she recognized me on a Sunday morning. Though she'd never spent all night with a screaming baby as

2

I had the night before, I saw compassion cross her face and spill out into her words. "How can I best help you?" she asked softly.

Tears filled my eyes. I was so grateful that she'd had the sense to ask. "I really just need to sleep," I managed. "I had a really rough night."

She nodded empathetically. "He looks like he's sleeping now. Can I take him for you so that you can sleep without worrying about him?"

Yes, that was exactly what I'd wanted but was too uncertain to ask. After all, she also had my three other kids to watch!

"That would be wonderful, Marli. Are you sure you can manage?" I said.

"Sure, no problem, Mrs. Kazsuk. Anything I can do to help," she said, quietly tiptoeing into the room and carefully cradling the contented infant. She left the room, making a soothing "shhh..." sound to the other kids who were following behind her like ducks in a row.

I closed the door behind her, my heart filled with thankfulness that God had allowed this time in Marli's busy schedule so she could help our family through this transition.

At eighteen, Marli had not only graduated high school but had completed her Bachelor's degree. Fresh out of school, she was just about to embark on another exciting project: illustrating a series of

3

children's books for a well-known author. Clearly she was extremely intelligent, talented and going places.

For many years I had watched Marli and her siblings grow in poise and character. While I knew these were not perfect kids (her mom and I are friends and have swapped stories), clearly there was something right going on in this homeschooled home.

These kids—and so many other homeschooling kids I knew—were inquisitive yet respectful, spoke intelligently with both their peers and with adults, and possessed a certain confidence that was neither prideful nor cocky. They were quick to serve, happy to help and, as a result, were trusted with responsibilities far beyond their years.

Behind these capable young homeschool kids were their intentional parents: the quiet heroes that had planned, prayed, sacrificed and given of themselves day in and day out in unseen and laudable ways. These parents too were not perfect, yet God had used their best efforts to guide these kids down the right path.

It was obvious that these parents had made deliberate (perhaps difficult) choices in guiding their children. The fruit in these kids' lives was not the result of chance but of specific plans and goals (and lots of prayer).

While each family's path was unique, it was evident that they had begun (and continued) their homeschooling journey with the end in

4

mind. They had dreamt big dreams for their kids, prayed for God's direction and guidance, and outlined specific goals for how to make those dreams a reality. Like a marathon runner with the finish line in mind, they'd diligently plugged away at their big picture objectives, trusting God to fulfill His plan.

Where Are You Headed?

It may sound basic, but developing an effective homeschool routine starts with the finish line in mind.

Twenty years from now, what do you want your children to have gained from their homeschool education? What are your long-term goals for homeschooling?

My guess is that your goals go much deeper than just teaching the multiplication table or the life cycle of a butterfly. Honestly, your kids could probably pick those things up over at your local public school.

So, in a nutshell, why are you homeschooling, and what do you hope to accomplish?

Some of the reasons why you've chosen homeschooling could include:

- One-on-one teaching

- Customized curriculum

- Teaching that moves at your child's pace

- Interest-led learning

- Separation from negative peer influences

- Ability to teach topics from a biblical perspective

- Time together as a family

What you hope to give your child through homeschooling might include:

- A spiritually-focused worldview

- A well-rounded, college-prep education

- Strong relationships within the family unit

- Strong moral character

- Leadership skills

- Ability to work well in groups

Dream about the type of education you'd like your kids to have. Don't stifle yourself! Don't allow your past mistakes or a child's previous challenges limit what you can dream up. We are starting new here, with a clean slate.

While some educational goals may be the same for all your students, don't be afraid to create individual student goals too. Consider each child's unique personality and abilities. When do you see them soar? What makes their heart sing? What challenges do you want to help them overcome? What kind of goals have they set for themselves (in the near or distant future) and how can you help them achieve those goals?

I love the mental picture of a child as a rocket and a parent as the launching pad and ground crew. We parents are given the first 18 years to shape the future trajectory of our little "rocket." What will we use to fuel up our kids so they can blast off toward their intended destiny with power and conviction? It's not our job to aim our child where we want them to go, but instead, through the wisdom of God, help the child discern his natural talents and interests and then help point him in that direction. It is our job as parents to prepare, guide and to lead them on their journey.

Schooling is how we get them off the ground and airborne. Schooling is the fuel that sets them soaring toward the incredible plans God has dreamt for them.

Relationships, Character Building and Real-World Learning

My schooling goals have dramatically changed since I first started out!

I shared previously about the number of homeschoolers that my husband and I have encountered. These kids— well-manned, highly inquisitive young people who were excitedly pursuing God's purpose for their lives—were the reason we initially decided to homeschool. My husband and I had decided that whatever was in the homeschool Kool-Aid, we wanted our kids to drink it!

Education and book-learning have always been high priorities in my life. Growing up, I loved school and got excellent grades. So, even though I had gone to public school (and didn't know any homeschoolers during my time in school) I was convinced that I would have no problem teaching my kids at home! It was just imparting educational knowledge to my own dear children, right? Armed with a good curriculum and a love to learn, I felt well prepared to give my kids the best educational experience possible.

With visions of national spelling bees dancing in my head, I saw my ultimate homeschooling goal as raising ambitious, high-achieving children that would be successful and happy in whatever God called them to do.

Then one day I asked a dear friend—who also happened to be a highly respected homeschooling mom—why she and her husband decided to teach their kids at home.

Honestly, her answer shocked me... and changed my life.

Focus #1: Building Relationships

"Alicia," she began, "We have only eighteen years to impact a child's life before they are turned loose to the world. Those precious years are foundational for the rest of the child's life, and as parents we need to make the most of every moment. I am not willing to give up eight hours a day, five days a week to someone else to make their impact on my child."

She went on to explain that "making an impact" went way beyond just teaching school subjects. Although she did her best to give her kids a well-rounded education, she stated that wasn't the main goal of her homeschool.

Rather, she said that "school" was merely a conduit for building family relationships and thus the relationships built during "school time" won her the opportunity to speak into her children's lives about deeper issues. Building friendship, trust and mutual respect between family

9

members were her ultimate goals because these opened the doors to true discipleship and lasting connections with her kids.

Focus #2: Character Development

Not only was homeschooling an incredible conduit for relationship building, she said, the hours and days spent together in the classroom were incredible modeling grounds for moral and character development and for Christian discipleship.

She explained that teaching character development went much further than simply making kids memorize character traits. Since more is "caught than taught" when it comes to parenting, she suggested that character development start with an honest assessment of each parent's own moral and character development. This takes time and lots of discipline but the benefits (both for the parent and the child) far exceed any cost.

Focus #3: Real-World Preparation

My friend also talked—a lot!—about how she wanted to prepare her kids for the "real world."

My first response to this was, "OK...I am doing this...I am teaching my kids how to read, how to do math. Check that box."

But it turns out she was also talking about a wide variety of things.

10

There were things that adults needed to know (that they might pick up in a classroom): how to take notes, how to prepare for a job interview, how to solve problems in a group, how to balance a checkbook, etc.

There were also things that adults needed to know (but that they wouldn't learn in a typical classroom): how to do laundry, how to cook for a dozen people, how to clean a house, how to be a good host, etc.

And of course there were the deeper questions of life (that many adults are still trying to figure out): "Who am I?" "What is my purpose?" "Why was I made this way?"

Clearly, preparing a child for the real world—in the way she was speaking of—went way beyond teaching reading, writing and arithmetic. That day I realized that God had built amazing opportunities into homeschooling—opportunities that, frankly, just weren't present in other schooling methods.

Are Daily Activities In Line With Goals?

Yes, that conversation opened new doors on the possibilities of homeschooling. But unfortunately, it didn't change how I homeschooled each day. Why? Because I'd not realigned my goals—and subsequently my daily schedule—to this way of thinking.

I still found myself pushing the kids through lesson plans and a strict, hour-by-hour routine that blessed quantifiable amounts of bookwork over the development of deep, lasting relationships.

Mastering a subject (often in the way the curriculum considered "mastering") was still our ultimate goal. I saw some bonding occurring between the kids and I, but how deep were those bonds? Were they deep enough to help us navigate the potentially tricky future waters of adolescence and beyond? And most importantly, were the kids being drawn into a relationship with Christ after seeing my daily actions?

Finally, several years later, I found myself—and my students—burnt out on school. They were tired of being "forced" to learn—and I was incredibly tired of "convincing" them that they needed to learn.

My husband and I didn't want to throw in the towel on our homeschooling experiment. We still felt it was the best way to educate our kids.

But clearly, some things needed to change in our daily routine. We needed to come up with some new goals for how to structure our school, and then to allow those goals to redefine our day-to-day activities.

With the end in mind, we realized that we needed to:

- Clearly define our homeschooling objectives (both our overall goals and any specific goals for each individual child); and

- Make an action plan for implementing these objectives. We prayed that a change in the focus of school activities would result in a change in attitudes regarding school (for both me and the kids).

Here's what we came up with.

Why We Homeschool:

- Customized learning that focuses on our children's individual learning styles and talents

- Concepts learned at each child's speed

- The option of which subjects to cover (and not cover) based on child's needs or maturity

- Character training/teaching about biblical concepts interwoven into everyday lessons

- Spiritual disciplines more easily introduced into daily activities

- School calendar formulated to dates that work best for our family's needs

- Free time in our days for relaxation, family fun and bonding (instead of time spent driving from school to school)

- Strong parent-child bonds and sibling-to-sibling bonds more easily developed

- Better control over negative influences and peer pressure, especially during the early, more impressionable years

- Difficult subjects discussed at the appropriate age for each individual child

- Difficult subject matter presented from a biblical worldview and within the context of our strong parent-child bond.

- Real-world learning incorporated into lesson plans and practiced in daily routines

- Field trips and "outside the book" learning available as we see fit

What We Hope to Give Our Kids:

- A close relationship with Christ and a complete picture of what it means to be a Christ-follower

- A strong moral character rooted in biblical integrity, perseverance and humility

- A direction and purpose for where God has called them in life

- A deep relationship and connection with us, their parents

- Rich, ever-growing relationships with their siblings

- Real-world knowledge in everything from how to cook and do laundry, to how to resolve conflicts and work with those that are "different" from them

- A comprehensive, well-rounded education in the traditional school subjects

- A life-long love of learning

(Note: These are our corporate homeschool goals, but we also included some specifics goals for a few of our children. For example, one of our children has some social challenges, so, under "What We

15

Hope to Give Our Kids," we gave this child the additional goal of "the ability to interact well with others, to accurately assess other's feelings and to develop strong friendships." If our children were older and were confident in their future career aspirations, we could also develop additional individual goals that would prepare them for that specific future.)

How Did These Goals Change Our School?

Our school now provides a high-quality academic experience within the context of the outlined objectives. A rigorous and engaging academic atmosphere is still high priority, but it is no longer top priority. Science, History, Math, Reading—these are the methods and practicums for learning character development, study skills and real-world preparation.

This means that I am now more concerned that my son knows *how to find the answers* to his questions about the Civil War than to memorize the dates and major battles of this conflict. This also means that my goal is to expose him to some of the greatest minds in history so that he may learn from their successes and failures as he travels on his path toward being a world changer himself_.

For our family, the knowledge and the subsequent school activities have a deeper purpose: what can the student learn about God from this? What new study or organizational skills can they acquire from the assignment? And how can examining this topic lead to a deeper understanding of Christ—his creation and his plan for mankind?

What has been the result of these changes?

While I would love to tell you that our homeschool days are a picture of utter perfection, I must admit that there are still mornings where when I have to summon my inner motivational speaker to convince my kids that, yes, we need to write that outline or finish those math problems.

But things have dramatically improved for the better.

Thankfully, our tough days are few and far between. I am learning every day how to let go of my ideas of "how" they need to be taught and instead allowing them to discover the information and respond to it in their own unique way. I've found ways to make school fun and interesting. Our relationships have dramatically improved.

I'm learning to slow down, to relax and to enjoy my kids through this process. Some days we stick to what's been planned for the day; and other days we "ditch it all" or simply follow a rabbit trail of learning.

I see all of it as the beautiful flow of rhythm-based homeschooling.

And what's ironic is that I feel like they've gained more book knowledge than ever before! I'm proud to watch them embrace learning and to happily dig deep into subjects.

Action Plan:

Before you go any farther in this book, I challenge you to deeply examine your homeschool's big-picture goals.

Ask yourself the big questions: "Why has our family chosen to homeschool?" and "What are our overall goals in homeschooling?" Write these as corporate homeschooling goals for all of your kids. Also write down any individual goals you may have for a specific child. On his graduation day, what do you want to have imparted to your child?

Stay at this step as long as you need to! Just like building a home starts with a solid foundation, take the time necessary to establish goals and set big picture plans for your school. The success of your homeschool rhythm (and of course, your homeschool!) depends on this critical step.

CHAPTER 2:

What's Working (and What's Not) (Part 1)

If you've set goals in the past and accomplished them all perfectly, you have my permission to skip this chapter (and the next one).

For the rest of us mortals, let's talk about the ugly side of goal-making.

Goals can be beautiful, precious things—lofty plans we make before we set foot on the path. They can seem easy—too easy—to fulfill. They lure us in with their wonderful promises ("if you work out three days a week, you can lose 20 pounds and drop two dress sizes!"). We convince ourselves that if we only meet these goals then our lives will be truly happy and complete.

We make our plans on the mountaintops, but oh, we must still trudge through the valleys. While joys do exist in the valleys of everyday homeschool life, the valleys can also be filled with bad attitudes, ineffective curriculums and overcrowded schedules.

Otherwise known as "stuff that's not working in your school."

Thankfully our homeschooling cycles come equipped with a summer break. This is our opportunity to climb back up the mountain, breathe the fresh air and grab a new focus for the year ahead. We can revisit our goals, determine what is working (and what is not) and continue back down the mountain with a new game plan. I suggest you do this every year as a healthy part of your homeschool routine.

But sometimes we get so off-track from our goals that we have to climb up the mountain much earlier than the planned summer break. We even may have to climb up there several times in a single school year. Life may have smacked us around a bit, or a child might be going through an especially difficult season, and we just need to be able to stand back and take a look at the big picture. We can't be afraid to step away from what's not working and take a hard look at what's causing all the frustration.

My Lowest Point

In early 2010 I found myself burnt out. I was tired of the endless pushing through the curriculum and fights each day to get school done. I felt like no matter how hard I'd tried, my children were still not the happy homeschool kids I'd wanted them to be. School became a burden and learning lacked joy—for me and my kids.

At that time we were schooling under a local public charter school and were required to meet with an educational specialist (ES) from the school every five weeks to assess our progress.

I clearly remember one meeting around that time. We were sitting outside a local coffee shop with the ES, school papers in hand. My students were not engaged in our conversation but were extremely distracted by the birds flying around the tables that were gathering bits of muffins and other pastries left behind by other patrons.

As the meeting progressed, my frustration level increased higher and higher as I listened to my kids' responses to her questions about what they'd been learning: "Huh?" "I don't know." "I don't remember." They continued to look everywhere but at her and it was all that I could do to keep them in their seats.

Toward the end of our conversation I finally gave up and let the kids leave the table and chase the birds around the courtyard instead. I was embarrassed by my children's lack of attention… and seeming lack of knowledge. I'd been working incredibly hard—perhaps harder than ever before—week after week to diligently teach my kids, and yet here was the extremely unsatisfying result of all my labor?

True, I couldn't expect them to perform like trained monkeys, but it was obvious that something wasn't working in our schooling. I'd seen further evidence of this in the previous weeks when I'd spent an inordinate amount of effort barking at my squirmy boys to "sit down" "pay attention" and "finish the workbook" while they moaned.

It was an understatement to say that this driven perfectionist felt shamed and humbled by homeschooling. And now my failures were evident to others outside our home (a school official, no less!).

While the kids chased the birds a few tables away, the ES leaned in closer to me and asked me if everything was alright at home. She said that I seemed to be stressed and that my tone with my kids had been "sharp."

Could this meeting get any worse? I thought. Now not only am I a poor homeschooler but a terrible parent as well?

Tears began flowing down my cheeks. "School has not been going so well," I finally managed. "I'm working so hard and we're doing all the assignments, I swear..." My voice trailed off.

The ES, herself a homeschool mom, sat silent for a moment and then said, "Maybe you need to step back and re-examine how you're doing things."

Yeah, duh! I wanted to say. Did she really think I hadn't thought of that? I'd spent each evening with my husband venting about my school frustrations and we'd yet to come up with workable solutions. The big questions were of course was what to change? And what to change it to?

I left that meeting feeling utterly defeated, frustrated and at my wits' end. I wasn't ready to throw in the towel but had no idea what to do next.

Over the next few days I spoke with several veteran homeschool moms about their times of greatest frustration.

Their advice was unanimous: I needed to back way off with school.

"It doesn't matter that you are in the middle of the school year," they explained. "You don't want to hurt your relationships with your kids or destroy their love of learning. That is far more important than completing the expected tasks and satisfying school requirements."

I have to admit that I didn't completely agree (I was still convinced that book knowledge was the main goal of homeschooling) but I trusted these women who'd been on the path much longer. I began the extremely humbling task of ceasing our homeschool routine.

For the next few weeks, I nursed my wounds and cried out in prayer. I was angry and disillusioned. Not only did I need direction, but clearly there were some deep hurts and disappointments inside of me that needed healing.

Time passed, and I began slowly introducing school again through games. Monopoly, Bananagrams and card games like Go Fish were brought out of our board game cabinet and into the core of our days. We spent a lot of time outside in our backyard and at the park playing. We read a lot (not "school-ish" books, mind you, but old family favorites that we'd read over and over).

I felt like I was re-introducing learning to my kids...and to myself. It was as if we'd had a cancer removed, and were now in the hospital healing and recovering.

I found a math curriculum that was completely workbook-free (Math had been one of our biggest battlegrounds and I think my forced time in the workbook had made this subject extremely unappealing for my kids). Very, very slowly we began working through a few sections with each child. On days when they could "sniff" that we were "doing school" and began to show signs of resistance, I backed way off again.

It was a slow and painful recovery but oh, I learned so much. Instead of forcing a "correct" method or style of learning on my kids (no matter how good it had worked for someone else), I learned to trust my kids' behavior and their responses to how I'd been teaching them. These were unique creations of God. How could I expect a prescribed formula or curriculum to address and meet their one-of-a-kind needs?

I also learned to respect their viewpoint and to value our relationship above any school task that needed to be completed. I learned to sense when I was offering them a healthy challenge that would stretch and grow their skills, and when I was just pushing them and needed to relax. It was a major turning point in my skills as a teacher, and as a mom.

Making Your Own Assessments

Whether we're going through a difficult homeschool time or it's just time for an annual check-up, we need to be honest about where our students (or where we) are, and then be prepared to make whatever changes necessary to make school engaging, productive and effective. Regardless of when or how often, it's critical to weigh the current health of our school against our ultimate homeschool motivations and goals.

At the end of the school year (or whenever your homeschool needs a fresh start) take some time to examine the key components of your homeschool. Look at each aspect of your child's current educational experience. Ask your spouse for his take on what he sees as working (and not working) in your school.

Specifically speaking, what should you consider? To get your wheels turning, here are a few questions (the Appendix has a more comprehensive list):

About the Curricula/Learning Style:

1.   Is real learning happening here? Do you see evidences of the child not only understanding the concepts but applying them in other school subjects and even in everyday conversation?

2.   Do you battle with a child to complete a particular subject, and do you believe that the curricula may be partially to blame?

3.   Do the curricula allow for the type of learning that you've chosen for your homeschool (for example, interest-led learning, literature-based learning, etc.)?

About the Student(s):

1.   What are his areas of weakness and areas of strength? What can you do to strengthen the weak areas?

2.   Are there core skills that you want him to learn by this time next year?

3.   Does he need assistance from outside sources (such as a tutor)?

About the School Structure/Routine:

1.   Does the time spent on school work for your students' needs and for the entire family schedule?

2.   Will there be an expected life change next year (for example, a new baby, a planned move, a part-time job for mom) that will require a change in the annual homeschool routine or in the daily hours of schooling?

3.   Should you consider adding additional out-of-the-home learning experiences, such as sports, clubs, or co-op teaching classes? Or do you participate in those experiences now and plan on eliminating them next year?

About the Teacher:

1.   Are there things about your teaching style that you'd like to change?

2.   Do you regularly exhibit the classroom behavior that you want your kids to have?

3.   Would you choose you as your teacher?

Make a commitment to do whatever it takes—reading books, talking to other moms, going to a homeschool conference—to discover solutions to whatever issues are present. This can be the hardest step, but hang in there! Real answers to your issues will be revealed.

Action Plan:

1.   Take an afternoon and think through your school's current status. Using the questions listed in the chapter (and additional questions in the Appendix), take an honest assessment of your school, your students and your teaching. Are you still on track with the ultimate homeschooling goals you've established?

2.   What are the hot buttons in your homeschool? Are there sources of ongoing stress, or of a feeling that things "just aren't working"?

3.   Is the curriculum still a good fit for your students? Do you need to examine new teaching styles and methods?

CHAPTER 3:

What's Working (and What's Not) (Part 2)

Next, I suggest you do something you may consider radical: Ask your kids' opinion about their homeschooling experience.

What do they like about school? If they were the teacher, what would they do differently?

Now you may be saying, "What?! Should they have that much input in how our school is run?!"

My response? "Yes, absolutely."

While it certainly would be easier if we were raising programmable robots, the fact is that our students are uniquely designed. They have strengths and weaknesses (those that are part of their personality and those that are present just for this life stage) and this affects how they respond to a teaching style or method.

We can make all the plans we want, but if those plans aren't working for our children, then what's the point? As parents we can ascertain a lot of what's going on in our child, but only they fully know what's happening in that gray matter.

When a manager gives an employee an annual review, doesn't the manager ask the employee to give a self- evaluation—a review of where the employee feels he is being successful (and where he needs to make changes)? The employee is often also asked to share any suggestions he has to improve the workplace or to improve productivity. Ideally, it's a two-sided conversation between the employer and the employee, with both giving input to determine the best possible working environment.

Shouldn't we give our kids the same respect and opportunity for input? It is their schooling, after all.

The End-Of-The-Year Date

Each year, around the end of May, I get to plan one of my favorite school days: our teacher-child date.

The kids love this special time with mom, and so do I! It's the perfect way to celebrate all the wonderful things they've learned this year and to verbally affirm how much they have grown.

It's also the perfect opportunity to get their honest assessment of last year's homeschool successes and failures.

Here are some suggestions on how to conduct your own special date with your student(s).

Invitation. About a week before the date, put together a fun invite for each child. You can go hog-wild here (if you want): a computer designed invitation, a handwritten invite, an email, a card, a scavenger hunt, a note with a picture of the child—you name it. Include the day, time and location of the date. If the child is older, you might also list some questions for them to consider as preparation for your time together.

Some years my invites have been fancier than others (depending on my time and creativity level)! One year I invited my boys to their end-of-the-year dates via two cleverly packaged gift cards. I purchased a gift card for the approximate cost of the date (I told them later that I wanted them to feel like "they" were the ones "paying"). I grabbed an actual plastic cup from the coffee shop along with a lid, straw and logo-themed napkins. I scrunched the napkins up inside the see-through cup so that it looked like the cup was filled with a yummy frozen beverage. I stuck the gift card in the middle of the napkins, put on the lid and stuck a straw through. Then, on the side of the cup I used a black permanent marker to write the actual invitation, listing the date and time. I did something similar for an invitation to a frozen yogurt place (filling an empty yogurt container with logo-themed napkins and the gift card, and writing the invitation in black permanent marker on the side of the container). Both were a hit!

Location. First and foremost, choose a place that the child would enjoy (hint: that place they keep asking you about!).

My five-year-old daughter is in love with our local cupcakery and gets googly-eyed when we drive by (I think it's all the pink frills and frosting...I get a sugar high just walking in the place!). So it's a no-brainer where her end-of-the-year-date will be this year.

For your child, maybe it's a frozen yogurt place, sitting on a bench at the park, time at the beach or other scenic location, or even a special "tea time" in the backyard. Wherever you choose, make sure the location allows for conversation and possibly has a table or desk so you can share papers and projects together as you talk.

Preparation. Make sure you've thought through your own assessment of the school year, particularly in the areas involving this student. Write down your thoughts and bring them with you. If there are issues of concern (and those issues can be seen in his work), bring samples so that he can see it first-hand. In addition, bring samples that demonstrate his hard work and be ready to praise all the wonderful things he has accomplished.

Most of all, bathe the meeting time in prayer. Ask God for ideas in how to steer the conversation; a spirit of openness (for both you and your child) that respects the other's point of view; ears to pick up on any potentially hidden frustrations; and wisdom for coming up with solutions to issues presented.

Agenda. This can be as formal or informal as you feel necessary. For example, you may decide to talk about one subject at a time or about overall topics that need to be addressed (or a combo of both). Here are some potential conversation starters:

- What was his favorite project or activity, and why?

- Ask him to list 3-5 concepts he learned this year. What does he remember most?

- Is there something specific that he would like to learn more about next year?

- Which subjects does he need to focus on next year?

- Are there current learning concepts that he doesn't understand?

- When and where does he feel he does the best work (a specific time of day or location)?

- What are his strongest subjects?

- Does he like the curriculum? Is the information presented in an interesting way?

- And (here's a convicting one!): would he recommend his school to others as a great place to learn? Why or why not?

Atmosphere. Praise, praise, praise the child! Although some potentially tough topics may come up, keep the tone of the conversation light and mostly celebratory. You do want to get his feedback about the year, and he will be much more apt to give it in a welcoming atmosphere.

Also, be committed to truly listen and validate any suggestions they give. I bring a notebook with me to write down any ideas (this helps convince them that their input is being taken seriously).

Of course, the process of getting a child's input can be much more informal than what I've outlined here. It may simply happen through a casual dinner conversation, or while waiting in line at an amusement park! There's no special formula.

Assessing and Filtering Their Input

Getting a child's input is critical, but as a staunch advocate of parent-led (instead of child-run) households, I do have to add three caveats.

First, the weight of a child's input varies based on their age and maturity. A mature 13-year-old's opinion should obviously be given much more consideration than a kindergartner's.

Second, it's also assumed that any seriously considered suggestions still line up under the overarching goals of your homeschool, and of the laws of your state. These two are non-negotiables.

Third, the parents' opinions should be given the highest weight of all. As full-fledged adults (charged with complete responsibility for the minor child) we make the final call on any changes that are made. We are the "employers," so to speak, in the employer/employee relationship. Even though employees are usually given the opportunity to share input, ultimately the employer has the responsibility to make sure that the company's goals are met.

It's important that kids understand this concept when asked to offer their input. My kids know that their opinion is valued and important. However they also know that, as they describe it, "If we each have one vote about something, Mommy and Daddy have ten votes!"

As long as these guidelines are not jeopardized, I highly encourage you to consider a child's suggestions.

Dealing with "Childish" Input

But I know what's coming, you say. *My child's "input" will simply be "I don't want to do math" or "I don't like school at all."*

Yes, probably so! Expect some of that! This is a normal response for a kid on this subject. I mean, if you were an eight-year-old boy,

39

wouldn't you rather play video games, build with LEGOs and run around outside than learn about the basics of English Grammar?

It's important that we listen to our kid's suggestions, even if they are...ahem, childish. Respect is a two- way street, and we can't demand it from our kids if we aren't willing to offer it ourselves.

But how can we marry their (perhaps unrealistic) expectations with the realities of what needs to be accomplished? While there's no perfect answer to this question, I'd say that honest communication (and an open mind) goes a long way.

Here's an example. When asked his input about Algebra and World History, your twelve-year-old says that he hates both subjects and would much rather skateboard instead.

"Ummm...OK..." is your response. "Let's talk about that further. Why don't you like these subjects?"

He shares that he's bored of always writing an essay for History (and that Algebra is soooooooo boring).

Here's the lowdown: Since History and Algebra are state-mandated subjects, Bobby must have them as part of his school day.

However, could there be room for adaptation?

Instead of always writing an essay for History, what if he switched it up sometimes and created a poster board for a specific History topic? Or what if he designed a video or PowerPoint presentation to outline what he's learned? Maybe he can focus on a specific aspect of history that he finds interesting (such as a historical figure or a specific event) inside the bigger historical topic? How can any subject be taught (and the information expressed) in ways that he would find most interesting?

Thankfully, there are oodles of books (and blogs) dedicated to making history come alive. Some curriculums contain fascinating activities and projects for each weekly history topic.

Pinterest is also an excellent place to look for ideas. You can follow one of my boards (I have many categorized by Homeschooling subject), or simply type in a topic in the Pinterest search box and see what others are doing.

And in the case of Algebra, perhaps he can try a different Math curriculum or method. There are so many out-of-the-workbook ideas out there. I've seen some amazing math concepts taught with LEGOs, iPad apps or literature-type books. Or maybe he needs additional help from a tutor. Perhaps it would be better if he did math first thing in the morning (instead of the afternoon, like he's been doing it)? These are all ideas for points of dialog to have with your student. Back and forth conversation (and opportunities for trial and error) are essential here.

And yes...what about skateboarding? Maybe you could dedicate time in the schedule for skateboarding or other activities your student enjoys. Perhaps participation in these activities could be conditional on him having the right attitude and giving 100 percent in his regular subjects.

Of course participation in the activity at all is up to you the parent. However, by allowing time for these "non-schoolbook" activities, it might demonstrate that his input is valued and that you do want to make time for things that he enjoys.

Also, consider the bigger purposes of your homeschooling, especially if that includes building close relationships within the family. Often the best way to do that is to include open, unscheduled time together.

Dealing with No Input

On the opposite end of the spectrum, you might have a child that gives no input or suggestions when asked about school.

This is a plausible scenario, especially if you've never given them a forum for input before! Some kids are shy about giving their opinion. Or, more commonly, a child may just have never thought about the details of what they do or don't like about school.

A few years ago, I discovered that sometimes kids (especially the "good," well-manned kids we are attempting to raise) can be experts at camouflaging their feelings about a particular school subject.

One of my kids clearly disliked our math program. His poor attitude and my constant nagging were dead giveaways. I also noted that he just wasn't understanding the concepts. So, when it came time for our end-of- the-year assessment, it was a no-brainer that we needed to look for a new math curriculum for him.

However, I was surprised to discover that my other son greatly disliked math too! I would have never guessed this since he dutifully did his assignments and seemed to understand the subject matter.

I think he didn't really know how to verbalize what he was thinking until I directly asked him in an end-of-the-year evaluation. So once I discovered that he too hated math, we talked about why things weren't working, and determined a new learning style and curriculum that might work better for him.

Putting It All Together

Gathering input can be wonderfully informative...and emotionally exhausting! Sometimes instead of clearing up issues, hearing additional viewpoints present new problems to solve.

Take time to digest all that you discussed with your students before making concrete decisions about next year. If additional conversation is needed on a topic, continue that conversation with the child before making changes.

You may also find yourself with more research to do: Is different curriculum needed? Does a subject need to be taught in a new way? Do resources for a new subject need to be discovered?

Although it may seem cumbersome to assess and analyze your homeschool in this way, the information gathered plays a critical role in determining specific goals for next year. Armed with the big picture goals for your school (and with an understanding of what's working and not working currently), you can accurately define next year's goals.

Action Plan:

1.   Prepare for and host an end-of-the-year date with your student(s). Come armed with a celebratory spirit and an open heart to listen to their input.

2.   Gather up all the information that you learned. Based on your assessments and the student(s)' input, what changes need to be made? What new resources do you need to discover? Visit Vibrant Homeschooling's "Recommended Homeschooling Resources" webpage for ideas (http://bit.ly/1yLeJ0P)

CHAPTER 4:

Determine This Year's Goals

"Tree houses?" I asked, surprised.

"Yeah, tree houses," my oldest son replied. "I think it would be cool to learn about how to build a tree house."

My son and I were on our annual "End of the Year Date," talking about what he wanted to learn about next year.

Hmmm... I thought of our postage-stamp-sized backyard and the definite lack of large trees with sturdy trunks. *Not a promising haven for tree-house-building.*

Next I thought of a recent conversation I'd had with my husband (while he was sweating profusely in an attempt to build a "simple" bookshelf) where he made me promise not to ever, ever ask him to do a woodworking project again. Strike two on the tree house idea.

I shared my initial thoughts with my son (why tree house probably equals no dice). Still he persisted.

He showed me pictures of several extravagant structures, some with glass windows and slides down the back. These things were amazing

47

masterpieces, many of them clearly not "built by kids" as the site claimed (what moron showed him that site anyway?!).

He continued to present his case. Not deterred by my "lack of sturdy trees" comment, he walked me outside and explained his vision for cutting into our slope so that the tree house could be somehow built into the side of our hill. "Who needs a tree, Mom?!" my excited future engineer exclaimed. *Well, I think the neighbors who live on top of the hill probably prefer we use a tree,* I thought.

Then he told me about how a family we knew had built bookshelves, chairs and even bunk beds—right in their own garage. I too loved this family (and had seen their mad skills with a hammer and nails) but at that moment I wanted to disconnect all their power tools and other assorted carpentry thingies.

Then the light went on in my head. Ultimately, it wasn't a fancy tree house that he was after! "Aha! You want to do woodworking!" I said.

He gave me a confused look. The boy doesn't know the term "woodworking," I thought. More evidence that the tree house idea is not a wise one.

"Woodworking... Carpentry..." I said.

Another blank look.

"You want to make things out of wood," I said finally.

48

His eyes lit up. "Yes, Mom! That's what I want to do!" he cried.

My homeschool mom brain went into action. Woodworking equaled measuring. Adding. Estimating. Dividing.

What other math skills could I eke out of this?

I'm sure the state department of education doesn't believe that woodworking holds a hammer to "proper" academic subjects like science and literature. But who knew? Maybe my son would learn a skill that would eventually become his future profession. Maybe one day as a husband he'd find no greater joy than building a bookshelf for his overly ambitious wife. Or maybe he just wanted to bang around with a hammer (as only a nine-year-old boy can do) and make a lot of noise (which was alright too).

Regardless of the reason, that day I said yes to the woodworking idea. It was important to him, and so it became important to me.

We agreed that it wasn't going to take the place of our regular school subjects, but he and I wrote "learning how to build with wood" as one of his learning goals for the following year.

And that's the next step in our planning process: crafting annual goals for each child. This is where you take all the input you've gathered (including the "I want to build a tree house"-type comments), lay them side by side with your big-picture homeschool goals and make some decisions for the upcoming year.

Setting Annual Goals for Each Child

I could make this section of the book really complicated and drawn out, but the bottom line here is you're going to gather up all that you've learned and make a good, old-fashioned list. You can make a fancy list (ooh...spreadsheets...) or a writing-on-a-napkin-type of list. As homeschool moms, we take whatever's in front of us (laptop or dinner plate) when the ideas, inspiration and time come available, right?

First, list out the subjects you plan to cover, making separate columns for each student. Start with the state-mandated staples— math, science, history and the like. Then include any other subjects that help meet your family's big picture homeschool goals (for our family that's "Bible" and "Character Training"), along with specialized subjects or topics for each student (this is where "woodworking" comes in). List sports, music lessons or other activities here as well. Write any notes about each subject such as "need new curriculum," "make a priority next year" or "ready for a challenge."

Next, write some quantifiable objectives for each subject, based on your own analysis of your school (and the feedback you received

50

from your students). This is where you detail exactly what you plan to cover next year. For example, you might write "The Middle Ages, the Renaissance and the Age of Explorers" as a history objective or "making outlines, and writing paragraphs and topical essays" as writing goals. These are the specific topics or tools you want your student(s) to have mastered by the end of the school year. As necessary, further divide these objectives into weekly, quarterly and half-year goals.

At this point, however, try to not get too bogged down in the details. We'll talk in much more detail about establishing a curriculum core and sequencing subject material in Chapter 6.

Suggestions for Setting Objectives

A quick aside here: I highly recommend that you focus on concepts learned, not curriculum or workbook completion.

In other words, it's much more effective to write "review multiplication facts, learn about fractions and introduce geometry" than to write "finish math workbook 2A and 2B."

Yes, write down names of specific curriculum if you know which ones would help meet the targeted objectives. However, I'm suggesting that a student's annual learning goals be tied to actually understanding the material versus simply finishing the book. You may have completed the prescribed curriculum and the student still doesn't understand the concept!

We have to be honest enough in our assessments to sometimes say, "That style or method didn't effectively teach the concept last year. This year, let's learn about this topic again, but take a different approach." This way, the curriculum becomes the servant to the student's learning needs, rather than the other way around.

Second, if you have multiple students, I suggest teaching the same topic to all of the children at the same time. For example, if you have five children, there's no reason for them to be studying five different history curricula! Why not streamline the process and teach the same history topic to all the different levels at once?

The entire family may learn about the Civil War at the same time, but naturally, each child will demonstrate what they've learned in different capacities based on their age and grade level.

For example, students may all learn about Lincoln's assassination, but perhaps a kindergartner colors a picture of Lincoln at Ford Theater (and narrates to you one or two sentences about what happened that fateful day on April 14, 1865 in Washington, D.C.); a third grader composes a sequence of events of that night; a fifth-grader writes a first-person account of the shooting (pretending to be the medical officer that helped the slain president); and a ninth-grader writes a two-page report about the reasons behind the assassination. This teaching style greatly simplifies teaching multiple children, and allows for the entire family to delve deep into a subject together.

There will, of course, be subjects that require different learning levels (math, for example). This is a necessary part of making sure that each student is appropriately challenged. However, if you're teaching multiple students, take advantage of every opportunity to teach the same topic to all the students.

Third, I'd also like to make the case for choosing one subject as the driving force behind the majority of your learning content. Not only does this allow students to really dig deep into a topic, it further simplifies teaching! It's natural to establish learning content around broad subjects like history and science because often learning objectives from several other subjects can be accomplished through one history or science project.

Let me give you an example. We're currently studying World War II as our history topic and the kids are putting together notebooks about each aspect of the war as we study it. A large part of our school day is spent working on these books. Although it is deemed "history time," it's clear that there's quite a bit of subject overlap: reading historical non-fiction and biographies; writing outlines from the material; writing paragraphs and essays; typing or handwriting; spelling; designing comparison charts and fact sheets; searching for and choosing photos, posters or other art for each page; coloring or drawing original artwork; filling in maps; creating event timelines; sequencing page information and page design skills; and so on.

Obviously, as needed, we also dedicate school hours to developing our skills in these areas (for example, weekly quizzes on misspelled words, dedicated time for learning about how to draft an essay and how to do illustrations). But I love how our history time is the practicum for so many other subjects. We're able to streamline, reinforcing so many subjects and skills at once! This is a more natural and complete style of learning.

Setting Your Annual Teaching Goals

And what about you? Did you come up with some things you want to change about you, the teacher? Ah yes, it's always so much fun to look in the mirror!

Frankly, much of our teaching skills are developed on the job. And the "required" teaching skills vary from homeschool to homeschool because we are each teaching a unique set of students in a distinct location.

That's why your goals need to be specifically tailored to your school and your situation. You've done some self-evaluation and gotten feedback from your students. Give yourself time to process all of this information and to pray for divine insight into how to best teach your kids.

Next, work to get your questions answered. Talk to other homeschooling moms; read lots of books and blogs; and give yourself deadlines for completing these tasks.

Some changes require little research but instead require a new commitment. Are you pledging to start your school day at 8:00 a.m. instead of 10:00 a.m.? Do you desire to take the kids on a field trip once a month? Write down these commitments and even ask for accountability from your husband or another homeschooling mom, if need be.

Don't be afraid to make mistakes and to try something new and out of the box. Unsure about a new teaching style? Give it a try and see what happens! So much of my learning to be a teacher happens by trial and error. And boy, do I grow from year to year! Don't be afraid to dump what's not working and to embrace a new idea.

It's September, and I Don't Know What I'm Doing!

Even after you've done all this, you still may not have all the answers. The school year may be about to start and you may find yourself more muddled and confused than before. Been there, done that, got the ugly t-shirt. Here's what I've learned in these times.

First of all, don't worry. No matter how much it looks like another homeschooling mom has it all together, I promise you that she still has unanswered questions about how to do this homeschooling gig.

Here's the greatest homeschooling secret of all—none of us have all the answers! Each year, all of us continue to discover each year how to be a better homeschooling mom for our particular family. Just like parenting or marriage, there is no pinnacle that we will reach where we'll have it all figured out.

Second, come to grips with the fact that homeschooling is HARD. As a homeschool educator, there's a reason why you get comments like "Wow, I don't think I could ever do that!" I'm guessing that people who are, say, trash collectors, don't get those comments. I'm just saying (no offense to trash collectors, by the way).

Find comfort in the fact that you are doing one of the hardest jobs on the planet (not only being your kids' full- time mom, but their full-time teacher). This is a tough job that not every family has been called to, so be proud and carry this calling with confidence.

In the seasons when it seems there's a lot of hard manual labor in the homeschooling "fields," keep your eyes peeled for signs of the coming harvest. You and I know the big-picture blessings of teaching our kids at home (otherwise we wouldn't have chosen this tough path). But in those moments when you need encouragement about why you're on this path, pray to be shown a glimpse of the beautiful fruit still growing underground.

Bottom line: just start right where you are with the curriculum and knowledge that you have. Start moving forward toward the goals you do have and the vision will begin to take shape.

Action Plan:

1.   Briefly list the subjects you're planning for each student, along with some quantifiable objectives for each.

2.   How do you want to grow and change as a teacher? Do you want to implement a new teaching style? Make an honest list of your homeschooling struggles and seek out answers either from a trusted friend, by reading a book or following a blog. Check out my blog's "Recommended Homeschooling Resources" page for ideas (http://bit.ly/1yLeJ0P)

PART 2:

Develop a Curriculum Plan

CHAPTER 5:

Create a Master School Year Calendar

Crafting a master school calendar is like putting together a very intricate puzzle. You know...one of those 1000 piece projects with little color variation and line design?

Overwhelming, taxing, and maddening.

Well, at least it can seem that way some years. Other years, it's like you're putting together one of those easy, 25-piece puzzles with your preschooler. Events line up, "puzzle piece placement" seems easy and obvious, and you find yourself done in no time.

While I can't guarantee that making a curriculum plan each year will be like that super-easy princess puzzle you may have done last week with your four-year-old, I want to walk you through a step-by-step process to make it as easy as possible.

One quick aside before we get started. No matter how perfect your curriculum plan looks in September, in June you may look back and realize that the actual school year played out completely differently! We can't perfectly plan for an unforeseen future, and we must give ourselves grace when the unexpected happens (or if we find that we've been too ambitious... anyone else ever been there?).

However, our goal here is to create a general framework of how the year might look. This will give an overall structure to our days and weeks.

Setting Up a Calendar

I prefer to make my Master School Calendar on a computer spreadsheet. Later on, I input key dates into a calendar program.

I like taking the additional step of writing everything in a spreadsheet first so I can view the entire year in one glance, then print the calendar as a one-page document. In addition, this extra step allows me to easily make adjustments and to quickly re-print out an updated master schedule for my desk.

I color code the weeks so as to quickly know when we are in school, when we are on a break, when holidays fall, when we have co-op days and the week number we're on for our specific curriculum.

However, if it's easier for you to work solely in a calendar program, skip the computer spreadsheet and enter the dates directly in a calendar program.

Predetermined Dates or Your Own Schedule?

Are you going to register your school with the state under a larger charter organization (the rules behind these vary from state-to-state) or will you register as an independent school?

When you register with a charter school, you usually are required to follow their schedule. This means you will start school, end school and take school breaks on the dates they've outlined. This is a blessing for many homeschool families (yes! one less thing to figure out!) and makes laying the groundwork of your schedule (the outside pieces of your puzzle) fairly easy. If you've chosen the charter scenario, this step is simple: plug in the school dates into your computer spreadsheet calendar and away you go.

If you've chosen to register your school independently, it's true you're going to have to sweat a little more at this step (more on the details in a few paragraphs). But for many families, crafting their own school calendar pays off in significant dividends throughout the year and is worth any extra effort.

I have schooled both independently and under a charter school, and there are merits to both.

While I don't wish to get into a debate about independent versus charter here, I will say, however, that if you want the ultimate freedom in your child's homeschool schedule and curriculum content, independent offers the most options.

Living the Independent Life

Our family is currently registered as an independent school, and right now we really enjoy setting our own routine.

We prefer to have a year-round schedule, taking a shorter summer break so that we can have several mini-breaks throughout the year. Knowledge retention seems to go way up, and my frustration levels seem to go way down. Being on our own schedule also allows us to travel to relatives' houses and visit museums or landmarks when everyone else is not.

We finally made the switch to being an independent school when I learned that I was pregnant with our fourth child. The decision was further cemented when we learned a few months later that I would need a Caesarean and thus would have a longer recovery time—smack dab in the middle of January.

I reworked our schedule, starting our Christmas break a few days before the holiday and ending it in mid- February. While a six-week Christmas break seemed ridiculous at first, I realized that it was exactly what we needed as we welcomed a new baby into our fold. With this new schedule, I had time to recover and enjoy those precious first moments with our newborn, and the kids were able to make up the missed school days throughout the rest of the year.

So, what are the additional steps needed to craft an independent school schedule?

First, determine the number of school days required by your state. This can typically be found on the state's department of education website, or via the Home School Legal Defense Association (HSLDA). My state, for example, requires a minimum of 175 school days.

Second, write in any holidays that you plan to celebrate. Maybe you take an annual trek to the zoo on December 14, for "International Monkey Day"? Or you're known as the family that hosts the "Bald and Free Holiday" Dinner Party on October 14? (No joke, people, these are real holidays!). Seriously though, you know which holidays are important to your family and your homeschool. Although we may just celebrate "Eight-Track Tape Day" on April 11 or "Public Sleeping Day" on February 28 (I'm just saying).

Third, write down any upcoming vacations, planned outings or other known upcoming life events. Are you planning a move? Are you pregnant or planning an adoption?

Fourth, are there any special museum exhibits or field trips you'd like to plan that are only during certain times of the year? For example, our neighboring town annually hosts a large Civil War re-enactment each year in March.

Fifth, write in any extra-curricular activities, including practice times, concerts, games, competitions, and the like. Perhaps your son has a music tournament next February in another state, and the following three months your daughter has speech tournaments every few weeks. Both require a lot of preparation and travel. Do you want to adjust the school routine during those months so that they only have "school" three days a week so they can spend extra time practicing and preparing?

Lastly, decide how you want to structure your year overall. Do you want to school year-round with a break every 5 weeks or so? Do you want four-day school weeks? Or perhaps your husband has every Monday off so you choose to structure your school week from Tuesday to Saturday. Maybe you belong to a homeschooling co- op and you'd like to line up your routine with their class days as much as possible. The possibilities are endless, so think about what would work best for your family. There are no rules except to make sure that you get in your required number of school days.

Enjoy this step planning and setting up a school calendar that works for your family! Just remember to keep some space, sanity and grace in your schedule (more on that in a few chapters).

Action Plan:

1.   Set up your master school calendar, either in Excel first or directly in a school planner or other calendar.

2.   Determine if you'll be registering with a charter school (and thus be following their school schedule) or if you'll be an independent school (and thus need to create your own school schedule). If registering as an independent school, plan your school dates accordingly, noting for holidays, vacations, upcoming events and other family activities.

CHAPTER 6:

Build a Curriculum Core for Each Student

We homeschoolers can be passionate and opinionated people.

Give us a platform we're zealous about, and we'll be more than happy to share our opinions to anyone who will listen.

This seems to be especially true when you ask us about curriculum and teaching styles.

We've all got our favorites, and boy we can't wait to tell you about them!

I have been on both sides of this conversation. I have been both the mom passionately telling another mom about the "ultimate" homeschool resource, and the mom who was just starting out, eagerly asking anyone she knew for advice on curriculum.

Nine years into my homeschooling journey, I am grateful to no longer be in either camp.

Of course I still recommend resources to other homeschoolers from time to time. And I am constantly dialoging with other moms about curriculum ideas.

But here's the key change: I am no longer convinced that a certain curriculum or method is "the best." I have homeschooled long enough to see all kinds of resources working for all kinds of different families. I have learned that no method, curriculum or style of learning is one-size-fits-all.

Curriculum Choices: Following the Crowd?

Some homeschoolers are so loyal to a particular schooling philosophy that they greatly limit themselves when it comes to choosing curriculum. They only listen to "the right" voices in the homeschooling community. They only teach from a suggested group of pre-determined books. And they avoid resources from those "other" publishers like the plague.

If this is you, can I please say (as gently and with as much grace as possible): Stop the madness!

The world is filled with ways to teach kids. None of them are perfect, but there are many, many good methods and resources out there. No one's got the magic formula!

If you're pleased as punch with your math or science curriculum, seriously, keep rolling with it. But I can almost guarantee that it won't work for all of your kids, or that at some point your current teaching method may not continue to work for this child.

It's just the way learning operates. Sometimes even when you figure out how a child is wired, it can still be difficult to find something that brings learning to life for them. And once you find a combination of effective resources, it may not work next year (or even three months from now) because our children are constantly growing and changing!

If we're going to rear not only smart kids but kids who fall in love with learning itself (which is the ultimate purpose of education), our teaching methods have to be rich, compelling and enticing.

My point here is to consider curriculum choices with an open mind. Honestly assess what's available before you lock yourself (and your kids) into another year with the "right" curriculum if it does not truly serve the educational needs of your child.

Take Time to Discover

Some curriculum choices are a slam dunk. You love it, the child loves it and you see their little minds grow and stretch.

Other subjects, however...well, they seem like that one cleverly crafted scavenger hunt clue that causes the most frustration and angst. Lots of thinking, searching and head-scratching going on here.

That's why it's important to allow lots of time for determining your annual curriculum choices. Solidify as many choices as possible, but realize that it may take time, effort and innovation before every box is filled.

Go to the homeschool conventions and walk the floors—yes, all of the areas—with an open mind. See what's out there!

Get on the internet and read, read and read some more. Discover innovative ways that homeschooling families are building a love of learning in their kids.

Talk to your homeschooling friends and gather ideas and input. Do they (or did they) have kids with similar needs? If so, what works (or worked) for them?

I do have a continually-updating page on VibrantHomeschooling.com with links to homeschooling products, curriculum and other teaching ideas that have worked for us as some point in our journey (http://bit.ly/1yLeJ0P).

However, I don't know each of your children's educational needs. And you may disagree with what I've deemed helpful because it may or may not work for your family.

That's why I specifically state on the page that although I can recommend these resources, we may or may not be using all of these products in our homeschool now because, honestly, some of them that did work in the past are no longer a good fit for us. Again, this isn't because the curriculum or method is bad; it's simply that I've seen my children's learning needs change.

Consider Building Your Own Curriculum

Many of these ideas will be eclectic conglomerations of all sorts of methods and techniques. In fact, you'll probably find yourself becoming an eclectic educator as you begin making your own learning combinations. The longer I homeschool the more varied my resources become!

It's exciting when this happens because it means that we are not stuck in the rut of who our child was last year or even last month. We are actively seeking to meet their changing learning needs. This results in knowledge that is fresh and exciting to hungry and active minds.

In the next chapter we'll talk more about creating this type of flexible, custom, "living" curriculum. In the meantime, let's begin the process of outlining curriculum choices by creating a place to write down the curriculum names and ideas.

Create Your "Main Curriculum Core" Template

Here's how to build a simple document to hold your main curriculum choices for each child.

- On your computer, open a new spreadsheet document.

- In the top row, type "(Your Child's Name) (School Year) Curriculum Core." Merge and center the box to fill four columns across the top.

- In the next row, type "Subject," "Curriculum," "Topics," "Frequency," "Teaching Time Needs" and "Shared."

You've now created a basic schedule template! Before you go any further, save the document so that you have a template to use from year to year.

Now, create a new sheet within the master document for each child, and fill in the same categories.

Fill In the Template

Now it's time to fill in the template with this year's basic curriculum information. Repeat this process for each child's curriculum sheet.

"Subject." List the subjects that this child will cover this year. To give a comprehensive scope of what the child will be learning, include subjects taught at a co-op and other extracurricular activities such as art classes, music lessons and sports.

"Curriculum." List here the main books and resources you'll use to teach each particular subject. Are you using the curriculum exactly as planned, or are you making some modifications?

If you're gathering together various resources to make your own or making major modifications, consider creating a separate document to detail this information (more on this in the next chapter).

"Topics." Although this document's goal is simply to hold a child's master curriculum list, you may choose to add more subject detail (such as "Addition, Subtraction" or "Marine Animals"). This additional information can be included in the "Topics" column.

If you wish to further flesh out a topic (by adding either additional resources or subtopics), create an additional document with more detail.

"Frequency." This is the approximate number of times per week (or the days of the week, if you know this) you'd like the student to work on this subject. How do you determine how much weekly class time to give each subject? You could base this on what the curriculum recommends, but ultimately, this is up to what you deem necessary.

"Shared?" This column's information states if the subject and/or curriculum will be shared with another student. This helps in determining how much teaching time (and preparation time) may be needed overall.

"Teaching Time Needs." Will the student work independently on this curriculum, or will it require a lot of hands-on-teaching? Can you teach several students at once? Does the curriculum require a lot of preparation? This column helps you track this type of information so you can see at-a-glance how much overall time you'll need to make this curriculum list a reality.

Take a Second Look

Now that you have all the information about the curricula in one location, re-examine your choices using the following questions:

- Have you covered all the necessary subjects?

- Can any of the subjects be combined?

• If you detailed a curriculum into topics, does the number of topics seem an adequate amount to teach this year?

• Do you need to create additional document(s) to further detail a particular subject?

• Do you need to adjust the number of times per week your child will learn a specific subject?

• Does the overall workload seem adequate for your student's age, grade level and maturity?

• Is the amount of independent work appropriate for your student's current study skills and habits?

• Are the demands on your time (whether for pre-class preparation or in-class teaching) realistic?

Action Plan:

1. Carefully consider your curriculum choices for next year. Are these the best choices for each child in their season of schooling? Will these choices help you meet your ultimate homeschooling goals? Follow the steps listed in the chapter to create your "Main Curriculum Core" template. Fill in the details about your curriculum choices in the document.

CHAPTER 7:

A Living Curriculum for Real, Live Kids

"Oh my, General," I cooed, in my best southern belle voice. "Do tell us about what's been going on at the front lines." I fanned myself with my daughter's homemade fan for added effect.

My third-grade son, clothed in his "finest" Civil War military gear, adjusted his military-issued rifle (otherwise known as his BB gun).

"Well, ma'am," he began, his eyes downcast and his countenance serious. "Some of the battles have been incredibly rough. That one at Gettysburg was really terrible and we lost a lot of men."

"Frankly, it was..." he began in earnest, and then stopped himself. He leaned in close and stated soberly, "Well, you ladies don't need to know the details of the horrors of war."

I laughed out loud, almost choking on my sip of strawberry lemonade.

"Mom!" he said, suddenly becoming my nine-year-old son again. "You can't laugh! We have to stay in character here!"

"Alright, alright... I'm sorry," I laughed. *How am I supposed to be Mary Lincoln when you're cracking me up with these comments?!* I thought.

We were seated in our backyard on an old picnic blanket. My older boys were dressed as Union generals; my daughter was pretending to be a woman of high society, and, yes, I was the First Lady (and host of our "strawberry soiree"), Mrs. Mary Lincoln.

We'd made as many "strawberry things" as we could think of (strawberry salad, strawberry lemonade, strawberry shortcake, chocolate-covered strawberries), dressed in our makeshift period costumes (my three-year-old daughter's outfit had a striking resemblance to a certain Disney Princess), and had a great time pretending to live in Civil War America.

This incredibly fun afternoon—easily one of the highlights of that school year—hadn't been planned back in September when we'd begun the school year. In fact, I'd come up with the concept only a week earlier when we had learned a random fact about Abraham and Mary Lincoln: they loved to throw a good party, especially a "strawberry soiree." In fact, the Lincolns were famous for these parties where practically every dish contained strawberries.

I had wanted to find a fun, low-stress way to review our five-week unit on the Civil War, and hosting our own "strawberry soiree" seemed like just the ticket. It had just been a bonus that strawberries were on sale that week.

I share this story because it exemplifies how sometimes our best learning activities aren't planned months in advance. Sometimes they just come together while the learning process is in motion.

The One-Size-Fits-None Curriculum Plan

My first foray into the homeschooling life involved a curriculum that gave a highly detailed list of daily activities (down to the exact pages to read each day). I was told that this was supposed to "free" me, because now I didn't need to create my own school schedule. "Think of all the extra time you'll have because you won't be planning daily lessons!" the curriculum brochure promised.

It all sounded good until I actually started going through the curriculum and realized that my family—or anyone's family, for that matter—could not perfectly accomplish the schedule the curriculum had laid out! Although the curriculum itself was challenging and filled with quality material, I found it extremely difficult to discern daily assignments because our days never perfectly matched up with what the curriculum had scheduled for us.

I'd see that there was a great assignment on Thursday for Science, but then realize (based on the flow of today's class conversation) how much better it would be to do it today. But the problem was that today was Tuesday and I was supposed to be doing something else today for Science. No problem, I'd say, I'll just switch the days and do today's assignment on Thursday.

But I quickly saw that I was switching assignments around on a daily basis. Sometimes I'd find a great idea outside the curriculum that I wanted to include too. I'd need to find a home for it in our weekly rhythm, which meant more switching and some eliminating. Then, as luck would have it, a cold or the flu would sweep through our family and we'd need to spend a few days off our schedule resting and recuperating. What happened to the assignments on those days?

Suddenly, I was asking myself, What happened to my "pre-planned" schedule? How is this giving me extra time?

Was this the curriculum's fault per se? Not really. While the curriculum wasn't my favorite, it had decent content.

The problem was that the curriculum's rigid schedule pigeonholed my week into an awkwardly-sized, unworkable shape. Like an oddly-sized garment that was loose in some areas and tight in others, this one-sized-all, pre-fixed schedule was clearly one-size-fits-none. I was tired of the extra time I spent tailoring this supposedly "time-saving schedule" to fit my family's natural learning flow.

What I really needed was a detailed subject plan that was organized and purposeful, yet flexible enough to allow for exploratory learning, last-minute project ideas and the occasional hiccup in our week.

Build an Organized Yet Flexible Subject Plan

It took me several years, but eventually I transitioned into a new way of organizing my curriculum plans. It has revolutionized our class time and brought so much freedom.

Instead of a moment-by-moment daily schedule of pre-determined curriculum content, I create a "Subject Plan": a document that outlines the general topics for each subject, and lists a range of potential activities for those topics. I let our days naturally determine the actual assignments.

Let's take Science as an example. Let's say I'm going to cover Anatomy this year.

First, I come up with a rough list of the content to cover such as "the Brain and Nervous System," "the Heart and Circulatory System," "the Lungs and Respiratory System" and so on. Preferably, this topical list would at least partially come from a main science textbook on Anatomy. I consider this main textbook my "spine" or "core curriculum" for the subject.

Then, using the dates from my Master School Calendar, I create an Excel document—which I title "(Subject Name) Subject Plan"—that lists these topics by our planned school weeks. Each topic and corresponding school week would get a row in the document. "The Brain and Nervous System" might become September 1- 12 (week one and two of our school year), while "the Heart and Circulatory System" is assigned to September 15-26 (weeks three and four).

Next, I create a list of the types of activities and resources that could teach these topics. Of course this includes my "spine," but it also contains additional supplemental resources. I create columns within the document to house each of these different learning avenues: "Supplemental Books," "Websites," "Online games/iPad Apps," "Online Videos/Movies," "Field Trips," etc.

Then, I begin plugging ideas into the schedule. This is where the treasure hunt begins! While a strong curriculum core provides much of the content ideas, I enjoy digging around to find other unique ways to learn a topic. So, for example, if I find a great online video of how the heart beats, I would paste the link in the column "Online Videos/Movies" in the row that contains the topic "The Heart and Circulatory System." The name of a pop-up book about the division of the brain would be filed under the column "Supplemental Books," in the row "The Brain and Nervous System," and so on. You could include as many additional details here as you like, for example:

"pages 14-18," "library book to borrow," "Netflix movie," or "buy this book on Amazon."

A Growing and Changing Subject Plan

The key here is not to reach a point where you state, "I have gathered absolutely every resource and curriculum idea for this subject." Instead, I prefer to have specific "gathering" periods throughout the year when I gather ideas in the Subject Plan document.

In the summer, as part of my annual school planning, I gather the core school books and determine the main topics we want to cover. If there's a supplemental resource that I know we will use for multiple weeks, I consider purchasing it as well. At this time, I also try to plug in as many ideas as possible into the subject plan, especially for the topics covered in the first month or two of school. Like a parent pushing a child on his first two-wheeled bike ride, these activities give me a good push toward what will happen this year.

A few weeks before we start a new topic, I intensify my "activity gathering" process again. This is when I look online again for resources, review the specific books available at my library and gather ideas.

Right before the week begins, I review what topic we'd planned to cover and the ideas I've gathered. I make an extremely loose structure of how the activities might work out that week: "On Monday, let's read from our core book about Western Expansionism in the 1850s and talk about questions on page 118; on Wednesday let's make a map that details the Oregon Trail and play an online game; on Thursday, let's build a covered wagon from an idea I've got on my Pinterest boards.

The week may work out exactly like this...or it may not! This is a general outline and if something isn't working, you can always switch in another activity from your Subject Plan that might work better.

Don't Overeat at the Buffet

You don't have to do everything on your list. Like the items at an "all-you-can-eat" buffet, you don't need to fill your days with absolutely every item from your Subject Plan. Really.

When my family visits a certain soup-and-salad buffet restaurant nearby, we're never quite sure what we'll eat. We do know we'll build our own salads and have the restaurant's tasty focaccia bread. But sometimes there's a great soup I want to try. Or on some occasions my husband opts for fresh fruit for dessert instead of his typical caramel sundae. It depends on our individual moods and what options are available.

It's the same thing with your Subject Plan. Give yourself lots of choices for what may work. Gather ideas throughout the year—the new ideas along with those tried and true learning methods—and pick activities as you go. Options are a good thing!

Most importantly, don't make it your goal to complete every project idea! Just like cleaning out the buffet is not the goal when dining at an all-you-can-eat restaurant, completing everything on your Subject Plan is not a true measure of successfully teaching a topic. Instead, ask yourself, "Did the child connect with the material in a meaningful way? Did they gain knowledge and express it in ways that will help them retain that information?" These are the true marks of successfully learning a given topic. Chances are that you'll eventually cycle through this topic again in your homeschool, and when you do, you can try those ideas then.

More Tips for Tailoring a Subject Plan to Fit

You can create these types of Excel Spreadsheets for each subject you cover. Or...not. Some subjects are super easy to plan and may just consist of working through a single book or curriculum without any additional outside resources.

Pick and choose the subjects where you really want to have multiple learning options. Don't make yourself crazy and do this for every single subject, especially with multiple kids!

By the way, if you are teaching the same topics to several children at the same time (but the children are in very different levels of their schooling), consider creating a unique subject spreadsheet for each learning level. This isn't really necessary for kids that are close in grade level. I'm talking to the moms with, say, a second grader and a high schooler. True, it adds additional complexity and work to make unique subject spreadsheets for each child, but it also gives specific options for all the learning levels present in your classroom which gives you freedom and choices for when it's time to teach.

Why a Living, Growing Subject Plan?

It leaves room for your kids' growth and new interests.

Last spring, my son enjoyed a short foray into watercolors. He attended an art camp in late March where he spent several days playing around in this beautiful art medium. So when we studied the Wild West not long after, he begged me to allow him to paint a western mountain scene as his main project for the history unit.

It gives kids options.

Your kids may not want to create a clay sculpture of the Titanic (even though they loved creating ones for the Niña, Pinta and the Santa Maria when you talked about "New World Explorers" six months ago). Kids can be weird and unpredictable in what they will like (but aren't we like that too as adults from time to time?). Having a plethora of options available to cover a topic gives freedom for those days when a child is particular about what he does and does not want to do.

It allows for last-minute ideas and plans to be easily added.

I find many of those spur-of-the- moment ideas online and Pinterest is an incredible place to gather and store them! You can keep separate boards for each subject, or even for topics within a subject. As you see great ideas online (either in the Pinterest feed or anywhere else), use the "Pin It" icon to add the link to your virtual Pinterest board. Then, anytime you need new ideas, simply open your board!

It allows for exploratory learning.

Kids come up with great questions and that can lead to awesome spontaneous learning ideas.

When we recently learned about the circulatory system, I'd planned to only briefly mention how everyone's blood is a different type. However, the kids were fascinated by the fact that we each have different kinds of blood, so we spent a lot of time on it that day. "What type of blood do I have?" they asked. "What about Nana and Papa? Do we know anyone that has Type AB-negative blood (the rarest type)?" We made a chart of our family and had a lengthy discussion about who could give blood to whom. The kids wanted to know, "How the blood got inside someone else," and if it hurt to give blood away. While I explained the procedure as much as possible, I made a mental note to take them with me the next time I gave blood (for a real learning adventure)!

It allows flexibility for planned resources that may not be available.

There have been many times that a curriculum recommended a particular read aloud or project book, but that resource wasn't available. This is especially true when trying to locate books through the library system. Sometimes there's a high demand for a book and it won't become available until after you're done covering the topic! That's when I look for similar resources or search my Subject Plan for other ways to learn the information. It's wonderful to not be locked into a particular supplemental book if it is not available.

Overall, having a Subject Plan provides structured and purposeful learning (important in helping us reach those annual or big-picture goals we've outlined) without the constraints of a predetermined, moment-by- moment plan. It is a living, flexible way to effectively organize and plan curriculum.

Action Plan:

1.   Consider how you currently organize your daily curriculum assignments. Does your curriculum come with a pre-planned schedule, and if so, has that been a help or a hindrance?

2.   Determine the subjects that will require the use of a Subject Plan. Begin listing out weekly topics and dates, along with the activities or resources to teach those topics.

3.   How do you gather and organize homeschool ideas? Consider using Pinterest as a way to categorize and sort projects, online games, and online videos. Vibrant Homeschooling's "Recommended Homeschooling Resources" page (http://bit.ly/1yLeJ0P) not only has learning resources our family has found helpful, but it also includes a link to some awesome homeschooling Pinterest boards.

PART 3:

Find Your Family's Rhythm

CHAPTER 8:

Rhythms, Not Schedules:
The Critical Key to Success

It was 10:32 p.m. on a hot Tuesday night in August. As the television droned on in the background, a Word document—my completed "Main Curriculum Core" for the upcoming year—was open on the laptop screen before me.

Putting this document together had been fun as I wrote down all the interesting new topics we'd be exploring together this school year.

And it was even like Christmas morning last week when the books had all arrived, each looking that much more inviting with their shiny plastic covers and crisp corners. Plus my kitchen countertop was now full of new notebooks, three-ring binders and dry-erase markers which only heightened the anticipation (some get excited about new shoes... and others about school supplies. I am in the latter group. Deal with it.).

School was starting in a few weeks and the promise of all that lay ahead was thrilling. There was only one problem.

How in the world was I going to teach this stuff?

And that's when the little voice that had been nagging at me for weeks was given a megaphone.

That's right... you're finally getting it, aren't you! You saw how this played out last year: drama, drama, drama. You've got all these great goals for what to teach this year, but how are you going to do it?!

My inner planner jumped into emergency response. Lists! Minute-by-minute schedules! We've got this, Alicia! You've come up with the plan. Now just make the schedule for it and implement it!

But somehow, I just didn't have it in me anymore. I definitely could put together a beautiful spreadsheet of my plans of how each day would perfectly flow into another (that's what I'd done in the past). But would it feel genuine? Did I honestly think pushing us through a schedule was the right solution anymore to getting to our schooling goals?

Some days it felt like a joke to have a homeschooling schedule. Math? At 9 a.m.? It was already 10:15 and we were still cleaning up from breakfast. And what was I supposed to do on the days when my toddler decided to skip her nap and throw a temper tantrum instead, derailing our afternoon craft time at 2:00 p.m.? These situations sound ridiculous now as I write them, but I know you get it.

The problem was I didn't know how to execute our school year goals without a schedule. And I'd proven in previous years that a schedule and a homeschooling day didn't always happily co-exist.

In addition, I'd deemed a homeschooling day as "successful" only when not only completed our assignments, but finished them in the pre-scheduled intervals. There were no in-between shades of "success" for me—it was all pass or fail. And how defeating it was for this driven perfectionist to tell herself "fail, fail, fail," on many of those days.

I felt angry and disillusioned because I found myself wanting a daily plan that was somewhere between the black-and-white extremes of "unschooling" and strictly scheduled learning times, and no one seemed to offer any solutions.

I've spent a good four years rebuilding from that point. There's been quite a bit of introspection as I've learned to see (and to appreciate) the middle grey ground between the mainly black-and-white extremes offered in most homeschooling circles.

What I'm offering in this chapter is my interpretation of that freeing middle ground.

It does require a routine (we are still shooting arrows at a target, otherwise known as our goal); but it isn't a rigid, hour-by-hour regime that causes stress for you (not to mention heaps of guilt) when it is not perfectly executed.

Instead of creating another schedule, this homeschooling approach focuses on a key element: the concept of a rhythm.

I know that at first glance that sounds like a minute distinction, but I promise that re-framing the concept from "scheduling" to "rhythm" can make all the difference.

You see, rhythm-based homeschooling still provides the comfort of a schedule, but unlike a schedule, rhythm works within the realities of an imperfect, unpredictable day. Rhythm is an achievable, grace-filled mindset that sets us free from the "have-tos" and "musts" of scheduling.

Rhythm says, "these are our goalposts for our day—the targets we're shooting for—and our day will flow around them."

Scheduling gives a specific time and place for an action; rhythm sets goals and says "my intention is for these goals to happen around this approximate time, but if it doesn't happen exactly at this time (or even during this day), then it will be alright."

Think of rhythm as having the same purpose as the wood framework of a house. Like a wood framework, rhythms give meaning and structure to the days' contents (what goes on inside the house). But even within the same weekly rhythm, different activities exist in each day of a given week (just like your neighbor's house inside looks radically different from yours even if you have the identical floorplan).

So rhythm provides structure without forcing the requirement (or the mental "confinement") of adhering to a perfect schedule. With rhythm, freedom is possible within the framework—freedom for late days, tired days, sick days, awesome days or whatever life throws at us. We can let go of the judgment and of labeling it not working out exactly as we planned and, instead, just enjoy the process.

Rhythm results in homeschooling drenched in grace, and gives our home educating permission to be a little messy and a lot more spontaneous.

If scheduling is a restrictive adherence to the rigid laws of religion; rhythm is the result of a passionate (and sometimes imperfect) pursuit of a living relationship with the Creator of the universe.

No Two Weeks Are the Same

Here was another radical concept that took me a long time to learn: I don't think I've ever had one homeschooling week that was exactly the same as another. Seriously.

I used to have all kinds of angst around this. Why can't I land on the "perfect" schedule? The perfect routine? I kept manipulating and playing with how to arrange our days... over and over. Surely if I could just arrange things exactly how they were supposed to be, things would flow like clockwork.

Without realizing it, I was heaping tons of inadequacies on myself. I was in this awful flight pattern: either fighting to keep us on our current schedule or I was promising myself to change "just this one thing around" for next week. My heart would sink at the end of each week when, darn it, something else would get out of whack and I was thrown back into the vicious cycle.

It was like I was opening a puzzle box every week. On the box cover it said that the kids and I were building a Spiderman puzzle, so I expected the finished product to look like a Spiderman puzzle. The kids didn't care what kind of puzzle we were building—they were just happy to be building it with me. We gathered up our pieces and began arranging them.

But it was like halfway through the puzzle, I realized that the picture being created by my puzzle pieces was really of Iron Man! The puzzle pieces all eventually fit, and there weren't any pieces missing, so the kids told me, "Great looking puzzle, Mom!" But I couldn't enjoy it because I was hung up on building a Spiderman puzzle, and only a Spiderman puzzle. Those middle pieces didn't line up like I'd pictured! I'd successfully met the objective of the time—to build a puzzle with my kids—but I'd counted it as a loss because it didn't turn out like I'd planned.

Do you get what I'm saying here (and that I'm really not talking about puzzles)?

I was so hung up on—prideful even—about my detailed plans for our weeks that when it turned out differently, I threw away the joy of the experience itself. I was trying to hold onto every moment and every task so tightly that, even though the end product of our week turned out beautiful, I was incredibly discontent because the process felt so uncontrollable and not what I'd planned for.

"There must on some sort of way to make this puzzle fit!" I kept determining. Really, however, I just needed to just put together the outside pieces and let the inside ones fall into place, accepting that however they fit together was honorable and good.

Thankfully, somewhere along the process my heart was awakened to the madness I'd created for myself. It was as if a light came on in a dark room and I began to see all the wonderful things that really had been happening all along.

There was so much goodness to celebrate: the kids were understanding—and excited about—learning incredibly deep concepts; they were making powerful connections between subjects; they were coming up with creative and interesting ways to express their new knowledge; and, honestly, they were just having lots of fun. Surely what I was doing wasn't failing them, even if the "center picture" didn't all line up like I'd expected.

I finally realized that my rigid plans were the problem, and that I needed to let them go.

I began making skeleton plans for our weeks and found them much more realistic—and freeing—than an hour-by-hour schedule that enslaved us and demanded perfect adherence. There was grace and freedom in a guideline that gave loose boundaries. This type of planning gave me permission to ditch a certain lesson plan if it just wasn't working, or to let the kids go off on their own learning tangent if that was what they wanted.

I began to see that my big picture goals were working out, even if the path we'd taken to get there was not the one I'd expected to take. In some mysterious, awesome way, I was keeping things loose and it was all working out beautifully.

I know now that what I was doing was creating a rhythm.

Rhythm-Based Homeschooling

If you get nothing else out of this book, my heart is that you will catch the homeschooling freedom found in rhythms. It is an incredible perspective that can radically change the climate and condition of your school. And I believe it is one of the secrets of homeschooling that no one talks about.

Why aren't others talking about rhythms? If it's such an amazing thing, why haven't others discovered it? First, I think it's because the concept of rhythms is fairly difficult to pin down and explain.

In addition, living in a rhythm-based state (instead of a schedule-based one) can be a scary place, and oh, it's so much easier to live in a familiar state (even if the familiar is unpleasant) than to step out of that boat and walk on the water. Fear often keeps people in the boat, even if that boat slowly filling with water and perhaps even sinking.

How could a mindset that brings freedom also potentially be a place of fear? We'll explore that (along with some practicalities of building a rhythm) in the next chapter.

Action Plan:

1.   Have you ever felt trapped by a schedule? Explain.

2.   After reading this chapter can you explain the difference between a rhythm and a schedule in your own words?

3.   Does the idea of living in a homeschool rhythm (instead of a schedule) bring fear or freedom?

CHAPTER 9:

Mysteries (and Practicalities) of Rhythm-Based Homeschooling

When it comes right down to it, we homeschoolers want step-by-step approaches. No matter the homeschooling label we give ourselves, the bottom line is that we all want comfort and easy paths. I know this because this is what I want. And I know it is intrinsic to human nature.

We want someone to hand us a box filled with pre-selected items and say "teach this in this manner and you will be successful," no matter what that method is. We want to have our teaching style figured out and nicely arranged in our minds before we actually have to teach.

We've sacrificed a lot in our decision to homeschool, and we don't want to mess it up. The actual task of teaching can be grueling enough. Plus we're also given the massive responsibility of parenting these children (not just educating them) which is an overwhelming task in itself. Not to mention that we have our marriages to maintain, households to manage, and our own internal and external health to look after.

So it's easy to think: Let's just adopt this popular routine or homeschooling style and go with it. We may not even realize (or take the time to discover) that an alternative, totally custom-made solution may be a better fit for our family.

And that's where rhythms come in. In spirituality, it's much easier to follow a set of rules than to instead be given a general framework of how to live and the responsibility of maintaining a relationship with a higher power. Like this higher calling of a relationship instead of a religion, rhythms require a trust in things unseen.

And therein lies the issue: rhythms can be frightening because the main powerhouse behind a rhythm is trust. To build trust, we must have faith in the thing we're placing our trust. And in the issue of homeschooling, that is a huge challenge because most of us have never been homeschooled, let alone ever served as a homeschool teacher before!

There is no ten-step program to the perfect homeschool rhythm. It is truly a day-by-day listening and adjustment to the realities of your kids and your life. There aren't any right or wrong answers and there are a lot of grey areas. I also don't know how you do it without a heck of a lot of prayers and trust in a sovereign God that works the tiniest details into the grandest of masterpieces.

It's a more challenging way of living the homeschooling lifestyle. And it does require going out on a limb at times. But, as I read in a greeting card once, "Why not go out on a limb? That's where the fruit is."

And yes, I must agree: the rich, satisfying fruit from homeschooling rhythms trumps any fruit born from a forced, static homeschooling schedule.

A Practical Look at Rhythm-Based Homeschooling

If you are willing to step out on that limb with me, I'll share about some of the more practical parts of building rhythms and hints on discovering your family's unique learning flow.

First, planning can still exist in building a rhythm. It just may look a little different than building a hard-and-fast schedule.

In terms of establishing a flexible routine, I look for two kinds of rhythms in our day: those that are fairly static, and those that change from week to week.

If we were to equate our day to a painting, the static rhythms are the broad brushstrokes of the painting. In my online video course "rhythm," we call these the "daily pillars."

The broad brushstrokes are the outlines of shapes, and thus the static rhythms are the most basic outlines of the day.

For example, on a typical weekday I get up at six o'clock, work out, then have some writing time. The kids and I meet at eight a.m. for Bible study, then have breakfast and begin the rest of our school day. Sometime in the afternoon we have a "rest time" where everyone does their own thing (quietly) for an hour or so. Dinner is served around seven, and the kids are in bed at eight.

The weekly and daily rhythms are a little more specific. They aren't the fine details of a painting (that would be more like a required, rigid schedule) but they are the midstrokes of color and shading. These vary from week to week depending on our commitments. On Sundays I think through the week and ask myself, "What's going on this week? Do we have a field trip? Family coming in town? Lots of a certain subject to catch up on? Or do I expect life to be pretty average and normal?" This helps determine how the rhythm of the individual days might play out.

I give the kids and I specific goals and tasks that need to be accomplished for the week, and then I give us permission to let those things happen in the most natural way possible. Within reason (and as my children mature) I give them freedom within this rhythm— meaning that I have some time loosely dedicated to a specific subject, and then I give them a rough block of time so they can tackle their assignments in the order that makes sense to them.

But at its core, that to me is setting a rhythm. I see rhythms as living, breathing entities that flow within: the context of our week's suggested educational activities; our planned or unplanned family commitments outside of homeschooling; and our children's ever-changing desires, creativities and interests.

Rhythms are the ever-changing heartbeat behind natural, child-led learning. They are the beautiful tension between our plans and ultimate homeschooling goals, and that of the imperfect, unpredictable occurrences of life. If we are truly able to embrace them (and not fight them), we'll see they bring variety, interest and adventure into our homeschooling.

When Hitler Hijacked Our Rhythm

A few months back we were studying World War II. You know, happy topics like concentration camps, Pearl Harbor, atomic bombs, horrific battles...and of course, the story of three power-hungry dictators and their quest to take over the world. On this particular day, we were studying Hitler, his propaganda and why it was so effective on the German populace.

We ran across several posters depicting the glory of "Die Fuhrer" (Hitler). But there was one poster that was particularly offensive.

Like many others, it depicted a glorified, triumphant Hitler holding a Nazi flag with a sea of soldiers behind him. But what made the poster over-the-top, even downright blasphemous, was that there was a dove (surrounded by beams of light) descending upon Hitler's head!

My kids made the connection instantly: "Mom, that's a dove! That's like when Jesus was anointed by the Holy Spirit during His baptism! What are the Nazis saying—that Hitler is a savior like Christ?!" So we talked about how, yes, over time the German people became convinced that he was their country's savior, following him in a cult-like frenzy.

We also read some of Hitler's quotes, one of them being, "I have not come into the world to make men better, but to make use of their weaknesses." We were all shocked at the contrast—the downright mockery!—Hitler was making of Jesus' statement in John 12:46: "I have come as a light to shine in this dark world, so that all who put their trust in me will no longer remain in the dark." We pulled out our Bibles and began looking up scripture after scripture that detailed

Jesus' beautiful servant heart—clearly a contrast to Hitler and his actions.

"How could the German people follow a man with such an evil purpose?" the kids wanted to know. I explained how they had been swayed by the Nazis' smooth speeches. This propaganda, along with a strong desire for national pride, forced the Germans to check their logic at the door. "It was a slow progression," I said sadly. Then we discussed how easy it was for any of us to follow the wrong path.

Armed with this information, the kids created a comparison chart between Hitler and Jesus (which they titled "Who Is The True King?"). It was one of those beautifully unexpected learning moments. They were excited by the project, and I was thrilled with the learning connections they'd made.

Did our discussion interrupt my intended rhythm for the day? Yep. That day "History" was more like an hour and a half. But look at the priceless, multi-subject connections that were made!

That day, we didn't get to Spelling and Grammar. I didn't have time to do my one-on-one Phonics/Reading time with my kindergartner. But that day I was willing to abandon these other subjects because the kids were lost in the love of learning.

A month later, I saw how much that learning time had affected one of my kids.

We were at a family gathering, and my older boys were asking their great-grandfather about his World War II experiences. When the topic of Hitler came up, I (tried to) share a few of the Hitler quotes we'd read. I know I flubbed the exact words because my eight-year-old, who had been engaged and astutely participating in the conversation, quickly corrected my quote recitation!

Alright, I was annoyed that my kid had showed me up, but I was also proud that he knew the info so well that he could correct me!

Clearly, long-term learning had happened here.

Rhythm's Ever-Changing Ebb and Flow

Every homeschooling day—often many times throughout a day—we're presented with rhythms that may be on the move. In fact, my homeschooling week is filled with days that turn out differently than what I'd planned.

It appears in a variety of ways: a child wants to try a different approach to learning a topic; or another child makes all kinds of excuses—some of them valid—as to why the deadline you've attached to an assignment is unreasonable.

Sometimes I find myself hit with an unanticipated twist in our rhythm due to circumstances outside of our control. I find myself frustrated at first, but then (thankfully) spontaneity takes over and the next thing I know we're in the middle of something amazing.

Yesterday was an example of that. Our Science co-op time with another family was cancelled at the last minute. At first my Plan B for this time was to continue progressing through the curriculum. Begrudgingly.

But then, while I was teaching, I was struck with a wonderfully complementary activity to our lesson on mollusks and shells. A few minutes later I closed the book (much to my children's surprise) and announced an impromptu beach visit to collect and identify the very shells we'd been studying. Screams of excitement echoed through the house. It was as if I'd announced that we were on our way to Disney World!

True, we had a fun time walking on the shoreline. But it also turned out that so much applied learning happened ("Mom—look I found a moon shell!" and "Oooh, look! I can see the byssal threads on this mussel shell!"). The sound of the waves also helped me out of the funk I'd woke up with that morning. Later, I was thankful that I'd allowed grace to alter the day's rhythm so that we could enjoy this moment.

And that's the beauty of grace. It gives rhythm permission for incredible, spontaneous learning. These moments can be the unexpected joy—the true treasure discovered—in our homeschooling rhythm.

Rhythms Need Boundaries Too

But rhythm-based learning isn't unlicensed grace in a routine. In fact, if left unchecked, too much grace in a rhythm can lead us away from our learning goals for the season. Sometimes we may need to say no to stepping outside the rhythm if we've found ourselves drifting off course.

Ultimately, we have to individually determine the "leash length" (or boundaries) we're going to give a rhythm, and that varies both by situation and day. To me, this is the sliding scale, or the grey area, between the extremes of "unschooling" and strictly scheduled learning times.

When do we give kids room to go off on a rabbit trail, or to even abandon a topic? And at what point are we uncomfortable with how that affects the rest of the day's learning flow? I don't think we can make hard-and- fast-rules here.

I feel that there are definite times in life—and homeschooling—when we need to push through and finish up a task (even if things seemed rushed or suddenly "scheduled" to make it happen). Perhaps we're working against a deadline, or others are counting on our completed work as part of a group project.

But there are also times when we parents start to force the day to go a certain way, and there's really no pressing need to do so. This is when we can ask ourselves, "Is it truly essential to finish this task today? Is it worth the pain and heartache that might result if I make it a requirement?"

You might decide that yes, it is worth it. Or you might decide that it's not. Only you can answer that in each given situation.

For me, it's easy to slip back into a "we must do this," (or schedule-based) mindset. I know this is happening when I start using phrases like "must," "have-to" and should." My stress level starts rising at the thought of not completing that particular task that day, and I find myself trying to force or manipulate the circumstances to make the activity happen at all costs. I find myself (repeatedly) saying things like "Hurry up! We still have lots more to do!" and "I know we've already done a lot, but we have to get this done!"

Or maybe you have the opposite tendency. If you tend to take a looser, more relaxed approach to homeschooling (and are frustrated that goals are repeatedly not being met), perhaps you struggle with not establishing enough boundaries around a rhythm.

We must give ourselves grace through the process, ladies. We must also give ourselves permission to acknowledge that from time to time we will be our own worst enemies when it comes to establishing rhythm.

At the end of the day, we are flawed human beings doing our best to inspire other (smaller) flawed human beings to educational greatness. Poor choices (and all the emotions that surround them) are bound to happen.

Perhaps the best comfort I can share here is that the longer I homeschool, the better I get at determining the proper amount of freedom within each rhythm's flow. We will never reach perfection here, but take comfort in knowing that time and experience allows the decision-making process to get easier.

Ultimately, we make the best choices we can in the situation and we trust that the Master Designer is making a masterpiece out of our beautiful mess. We walk in faith that He alone is sovereign over the ultimate outcome of our rhythms. This gives me comfort—and freedom to fail—when I'm faced with finding my way through a changing rhythm.

Action Plan:

1.   Do you find comfort in following a pre-determined homeschool method? If so, has that method also brought confinement and rigidity?

2.   In what ways have you recently witnessed the ebb and flow of your family's homeschool rhythm?

3.   Have you seen positive moments in your homeschooling when you followed the unexpected pattern of a rhythm?

4.   Have you experienced moments where you felt that a rhythm overstepped its boundaries and led the family off track for the season's learning goals?

CHAPTER 10:

Consider Your Unique Learning Environment

One of the greatest challenges of homeschooling is that your children are continually growing and changing—and so is your homeschooling environment! Some of these changes can be anticipated. Others are completely unexpected and out of your control.

Homeschooling doesn't exist in a vacuum—it revolves around real life! Therefore, all the planning in the world is meaningless if it isn't developed within the daily reality of life situations like extracurricular activities, household tasks or other responsibilities. If not considered in the overall rhythm, each of these scenarios can throw a major curveball into a homeschool routine. That's why it's critical to identify outside challenges to homeschooling and discuss strategies to encourage smooth and easy rhythms.

Challenges Outside of School

Let's talk about real homeschool life for a moment, shall we?

Squirmy kids who can't sit still for more than 5 minutes. Babies and toddlers who need extra attention. Younger students who need mom's full attention for nearly all their assignments. One-on-one, complex instruction for older students in advanced subjects. Students that zone out in the afternoons. (Enter your homeschooling challenges here).

To top it all off, each of these kids are on their own unique learning path—with their own curriculum lists and extracurricular activities!

Situations like these are the mainstays of homeschool life (although that doesn't make them any easier!). Every homeschool has distinct challenges—some more than others. This is what makes your learning environment unique from mine.

While it's impossible to identify and discuss every possible challenge, let's look at those listed above and talk through some strategies.

Challenge # 1: Each Child's Routine Is Different

This is the foundational challenge that we must all address if we have multiple children.

Consider this hypothetical example: This year, Todd's tenth grade subjects include Science, History, Writing, Philosophy, Grammar, Math, Speech/Debate, and Literature (plus violin lessons). Betsy's sixth grade subject list also includes Science, History, Math and Writing (which she will do at the same time as Todd), but she also has

Spanish, Cursive Writing, Spelling and an outside Art class. And then there's six-year-old Cayden. He has Phonics, Handwriting, Spelling, Math, History, Science and Karate twice a week.

Bottom line: everyone's individual learning path must be considered when determining an approximate daily school rhythm for the family.

In Chapter 3, we discussed outlining unique goals for the year for each child. While there's hopefully some subject overlap (the benefits of this are also discussed in Chapter 3), each child is going to be following his own learning trajectory.

In addition, consider the routines of any non-school aged children as well. While baby Jillian may not be a student yet, her life does follow a pattern that interacts with how the rest of your school day happens (we'll talk more about that below in "Challenge #3: Babies and Toddlers).

Challenge #2: Squirmy Kids

Granted, this seems to mainly strike those with younger kids, but some of us have older children with attention disorders that are also plagued with the squirmies. Some kids are just kinesthetic learners and need to move around a lot.

Here's how I've handled it in our school. When considering how to arrange the order of a "squirmy" child's school day, I try to alternate between independent, solitary activities (writing, independent reading and bookwork) and physical, social activities (an interactive class game, one-on-one time with a sibling, free play in the backyard).

I don't go crazy and try to force a rhythm to perfectly fit like this every day. I just try to keep this concept of alternating between independent/solitary and physical/social activities as I see the day playing out.

I've mentally accepted that this type of learner needs lots of scheduled breaks, especially after he's been asked to sit down for a while. If the child starts acting out, I consider if we need to break the day into smaller chunks, perhaps switching topics every thirty minutes or so (or more frequently if the child is both young and naturally squirmy).

Challenge #3: Babies and Toddlers

When it comes to homeschooling with a baby in the house, one blessing is that most babies take a least one nap a day. Of course each day is different, but I try to arrange our routine so that we get as much done as possible during the baby's nap time. In fact, I specifically attempt to do the school activities that require my one-on- one coaching during the younger one's nap times.

But, oh, the dreaded days when babies grow into toddlers and then preschoolers, all the while slowing outgrowing their need for naps! Don't get me wrong—this is a precious childhood age and a wonderful parenting time to savor. It's just not the easiest stage when you're also trying to homeschool.

When naptime is no longer a viable option for taking care of the "meatier" parts of a homeschool day, consider these ideas.

First, it may work to schedule time for an older sibling to play with the toddler or preschooler. Not only is the younger child thrilled to have a dedicated playmate, the older child is learning responsibility, humility, and an others-focused attitude. In addition, priceless bonds are being built between the children (which may be one of your main reasons for homeschooling in the first place). Present this time as a wonderful reward for the older child (now they are old enough to be a helper with the younger kids!) and remind him that this is an extra "break" in his school studies. Set aside a special box of toys and games only to be used for this time together.

Another idea is to designate a corner of the school area for this little one and give him some special, age- appropriate activities that only come out during school time. These activities could be specially set-aside toys. Some moms make "busy bags,": homemade sorting, coloring and stacking-type games gathered together from simple household objects. Oodles of busy bag ideas abound on the internet, (and I have a few on my Pinterest "Homeschooling: Toddler Learning and Busy Activities" board). Along with teaching a young child important skills like focusing, listening and paying attention, some

123

busy bag activities encourage early literacy and number skills. This time of independent quiet play is also important for a child's social development because the child learns at an early age not to expect to always be entertained by others.

Challenge #4: Students That Need Lots of One-On-One Teaching

There could be several reasons for this: the student may be very young and not literate yet (and therefore can't read his own assignments); the student may be older and needs adult perspective and interaction with a difficult subject; a student of any age may find a subject challenging and therefore requires additional teacher instruction time; or the curriculum may require lots of active teaching time.

Obviously we moms can't be in two places at once! If you know in advance that you'll have one or two children that fall into the above categories, consider ways to arrange your teaching time so that you are available to help when needed. Don't plan to do your daughter's high-need-teaching subject in the same time-slot as your five-year-old son who is unable to read. Examine one student's routine against another to create the best possible rhythm for the whole family.

However, I've come to realize that sometimes a child needs me to help them through a difficult task, and there is just no way to predict this! It can be difficult, but I do my best to give myself and the kids grace at these times. While I encourage my kids to figure out as much as possible on their own, I always give them the option of asking me for help should they need it.

Challenge #5: Natural Biorhythms

Like any other human, your students probably have segments of their day when their minds are fresh and active, and other segments when they're simply ready to shut down for a while. Call it our body's natural biorhythms, the two o'clock doldrums, or simply the inability for students to focus late in the day. Regardless, consider how you can work with (and not against) these biologically based learning ebb and flows.

First, consider how a student's dietary intake affects his ability to learn. If a child eats sugary cereals (or a breakfast without a lot of protein or complex carbohydrates), no wonder he gets that deer-in-the-headlights look around 10 a.m.! A quick blood sugar spike and drop can result in fatigue and a reduced attention span. Consider what your child eats and when he eats it. Maybe it's time to reformulate breakfast, to add a morning snack or to change up the family's typical lunch. This could make a huge difference in a child's attention span.

Also, did you know that drinking water wakes up the brain and prepares you to learn? Seriously—when I'm feeling groggy or unfocused (or my child seems to be) I ask myself "when did I (or the child) last drink water?"

Challenge #6: Scheduled Activities Outside the Home

You may have regular, planned activities such as sports, music lessons or outside classes with other homeschoolers. Maybe you have a mom's group that you lead every Wednesday morning, or a part-time job may be part of your weekly routine. Regardless of the situation, school may be limited on these days and heavy on others. It's all good. This is just part of your family's rhythm for this season!

For example, when I was pregnant with my fourth baby, my prenatal visits were on Fridays, so we did most of our school from Monday to Thursday and left Friday mornings open. This only lasted for the last six weeks of the pregnancy, but being aware of this small change in Friday morning's rhythm allowed me to not feel so de- railed on those days.

Challenge #7: Unscheduled Activities (AKA Real Life)

This is a challenge that we all share! Kids get sick. A friend may need your help at the last minute. It's just the way life works. And my goodness, it's what makes each day unique and beautiful from the other.

Each day has challenges that we could never predict or plan for. Sometimes when we hold onto the reins of our routine too tightly, it's easy to get upset at life's little hiccups.

The best way I've found to deal with this is to approach each week not with rigid plans, but loose intentions. If an unexpected situation presents itself in a given day , I ask myself, "What would I like to get done for this day? Are there things that I would consider a higher priority than others?"As a result, some activities or tasks get bumped off the list for the day. I recognize that, even with the truest intentions and the greatest effort, sometimes these tasks just won't get done, so I try to remove any expectations around them.

Of course this is so much easier said than done because we attach emotions to our tasks (for me, it's guilt and overwhelm when certain tasks aren't completed).

Slowly but surely however, I'm learning to practice grace with myself: grace that sometimes I just won't get it all done, despite my best intentions. I'm beginning to trust that there must have been other purposes for me that day: for example, to show compassion to an ill child; to practice my patience as I sit for an extra long time at a doctor's office; or to offer encouragement to a friend in need. It can be difficult to accept in the moment, but in the grand scheme of things, these activities are also a valuable use of our time because they shape our character (and that of our kids).

127

Challenge # 8: What, You Have a House to Run Too?

Ah, yes... if only we could homeschool without the added "home" responsibilities. Those darn dishes just keep piling up while we're happily doing science experiments and creating salt dough relief maps.

I long to be one of those moms that vacuums her house from 5:00 to 5:30 on Wednesdays evenings and cleans her bathrooms every other Tuesday. However, I just don't find my life to be that predictable from week to week.

But this doesn't mean that my family and I completely abandon the idea of incorporating household tasks into our daily rhythm.

What seems to work for us is to create open spaces in our week where these kinds of activities are possible. For our family, that's the late afternoons and right before dinner. Most days, I purposely leave these times fairly open so that if the bathrooms really need cleaning or we need to tidy up because we're having dinner guests, we can use that time without it impacting our school day too much.

We also try to keep regular routines for some of the basic chores (dishes in the morning and afternoon; and laundry on Sunday, Monday and Tuesday, for example).

But no matter when the jobs get done, my husband and I are firm believers in complete family involvement in the household tasks. We train our kids to do the task while we're doing it ourselves and then slowly hand over the reins so that eventually they can do the task on their own. I've learned not to expect perfection, but to appreciate the effort given based on the child's age. We offer lots of grace here with them (and, yes, lots of practice) so that they feel like whatever work they are doing is meaningful and helpful (which it is).

However, there are certain activities that I incorporate into our month that truly are lifesavers in maintaining our rhythm. For me, those are meal planning, once-a-month grocery shopping and freezer meals.

Keep On Trucking

If you're feeling overwhelmed after reading all of these challenges, take a deep breath and know that you are in great company.

I find that giving myself grace around these things is critical. I remind myself that I'm giving my all (and truly, so are my kids). Therefore, I constantly give us permission to have days that don't work out as planned.

And remember—sometimes a day gets off kilter and doesn't turn out for the worse, but somehow turns out even better than anticipated!

These are complicated issues that take time and creativity to solve. Don't let them bog you down or cause more stress. Just keep them in mind as you're trying to anticipate the family's homeschool rhythm for a given week.

Action Plan:

1. Think through your school's unique challenges. What strategies would be helpful in keeping your rhythm as smooth as possible?

2. Do you need to do additional research to get workable solutions to these issues? Or do you feel as if you're running as efficiently as you can and you just need to give yourself more grace and permissions around these areas?

3. How do household responsibilities affect your family's homeschool routine? If so, take a second look at the systems you may (or may not) have in place to handle these everyday tasks. What feels more comfortable: to create a more formal plan to manage these tasks, or to allow yourself and your family more grace in this area during this busy season? Are there areas where the children can offer additional help?

CHAPTER 11:

When Life Interrupts Your "Perfect" Rhythm

On a Tuesday in late winter 2008, my eyes opened to the morning light. As my brain woke up and began thinking through the day, I suddenly remembered: *today's my birthday!*

I was still laying on my back, adrift in the pleasure of the moment (*It's my birthday! My BIRTHDAY!*) when I heard a little voice from the side of the bed.

"Momma, I itchy," it said simply.

I sat up and found my three-and-a half-year-old covered in angry, bright-red blotches and puffed up like a marshmallow.

I nudged my still-sleeping husband (well, he probably woke up when he heard me gasp and shout "Oh my gosh!" at the sight of our son).

Incredulous, we both sat there with our mouths open as we stared our son. *What in the world?!*

As we examined him more closely, fully awake now, we began going through the scenarios: No one we knew had chicken pox. It had been cold lately, so the kids had barely been outside, let alone played near bushes that might have caused a rash.

And then we noticed he wasn't breathing well either. Gasping and wheezing was more like it. Not quite call-911-status, but definitely not normal.

We immediately called the doctor. We were told to bring him in right away.

That was the day we discovered he was allergic to penicillin. An emergency visit to the doctor, a child covered in a strange, scary rash, and then a lesson in how to apply an oxygen mask to a three-and-a-half-year-old. Yeah, not exactly how I'd dreamt of spending my birthday.

Or the next seven days. We spent almost every day that week at the doctor's office as the allergic reaction—and the subsequent hives, swelling and wheezing—raged through his poor little body. He'd been on penicillin for eight days before showing signs, so it took a very long time for the symptoms to pass. There were several times in that week when we almost admitted him to the hospital. When we weren't at the doctor or at home pumping him full of Benadryl, we kept him in a cool bath—basically the only thing that kept the itching moderately at bay.

My sweet, mellow boy was exhausted mentally and physically and just wanted it to be over. After five days of this craziness, one afternoon he just began crying uncontrollably. I held him close, tears streaming down my cheeks too. He was a wreck, and so was I.

I think it goes without saying that we did very little homeschool that week. In fact, I think the only "school" I did was reading a few stories aloud while sitting at the doctor's office.

This situation wasn't planned and it wasn't ideal. But, unfortunately, it was our reality that week.

Now That's One Upset Apple Cart

While we do our best to prepare for life's interruptions, they still can be sudden, jarring and life-altering.

Sometimes they last for a day or for a week. And sometimes they last for the entire school year (or longer).

Here are a few examples of those "big" interruptions that can rock your world (and your homeschooling rhythm):

- Your husband just lost his job and you need to get a part-time job as soon as possible (while still homeschooling your children).

- Your teenage nephew just committed suicide and your sister is beside herself with grief.

- A tornado ripped through your town yesterday afternoon, severely damaging your home.

- Your mother-in-law is moving in due to a recent stroke.

- You just learned that your neighbor has Stage 3 Breast Cancer and you offered to help watch her kids three days a week.

How are we expected to maintain any semblance of a routine during these challenging times?

Ever heard the phrase, "The baby is the lesson"? It means that the real lesson to be learned in a given situation is found in the very thing that is causing the disruption.

I'm grateful that my family has not endured enormously difficult situations like the ones stated above. However, we have gone through many small speed bumps where I have seen this "the baby is the lesson" principle repeatedly ring true. These difficulties may only last for a day at a time, but they repeat themselves over and over, making me ask myself, "Am I stuck in Groundhog Day (remember that old Bill Murray movie)? Geez, can I just learn the lesson already?!"

As teachers, we tend to forget that we are students too! Sometimes we have to be shaken from our boxed-in routines so that growth and change can happen.

Instead of being angry and frustrated about our upset little apple cart, what if we stepped back from the situation and asked ourselves, "What can I (and my kids) learn in this situation? What unique life lessons are available here?"

All of this is to say that "interruptions" to the routine—planned or unplanned—have a purpose, and that growing time for us is often a growing time for our kids as well.

While this growing time may not be traditional textbook learning, these experiences are invaluable and just as educational! Remember— they help accomplish those big-picture goals that you just can't find a textbook for: stuff like developing family connections, building character and cultivating necessary life skills. It can be a challenge, but do your best to roll with the punches and look for the lesson.

Time for a New Lesson Plan

In spring of 2012, my mom needed to have an unexpected surgery. My dad wasn't able to take any time off work. My sister, my only sibling,

135

lives five minutes from my mom, but she also works full-time. It was smack dab in the middle of our school year, my parents live more than two hours away and, quite frankly, our schedule was fairly full. But I knew my mom would need help, and I saw a unique opportunity to teach my kids about the importance of service.

So we decided to completely change our homeschool rhythm (and all our plans) for the week. My four-year-old daughter, my still-nursing infant son and I traveled to my mom's house and set up camp. The older boys stayed behind with my husband who had dramatically lightened his workload so he could work from home that week.

While we were gone, the boys still maintained a very loose homeschool framework—Bible in the morning, Math, and lots of independent reading.

And my daughter? Well, as a child blessed with a compassionate spirit, she is always quick to offer a Band Aid and a hug to anyone in need. So, her homeschooling for the week simply consisted of using her talents. This was real-world, applied learning—for a preschooler!

These unscheduled opportunities are some of the greatest beauties in homeschooling. They remind me of the Bible story of the Good Samaritan (Luke 10:30-37). We've got to be open to learning opportunities happening outside our regular school rhythms.

Character Development Won't Keep a Schedule

Recently the kids and I were getting ready for an all-day field trip. My older sons were finishing up some math before we left, and my daughter and I were in the kitchen. I was gathering up sunscreen and other last-minute items. Lunches still needed to be made, and we were running behind schedule.

My daughter was also supposed to be doing math, but since she had very little math to do that day, I decided it would be most beneficial if she could help me with the lunches. In that moment, I saw burrito-making as a spontaneous opportunity for character building (math could be done when we returned from the field trip).

My usually helpful daughter gave me a look. One of those looks. "Do I have to make burritos for the boys too?"

"Yes, please," I said. "It would really help us get out the door faster." She still was not convinced. "What am I, their servant?" she said, in an irritated, arrogant tone.

Her response shocked me out of my bustling around. Oh, yes. This was definitely one of those time-sensitive teaching moments. Summoning up my patience (and doing my best to respond gently with a controlled tongue), I crouched down so that we were at eye level. "Yes, exactly. You are their servant."

137

I paused. I could tell by her eyes that she was surprised at my response.

I continued. "I am your servant, and you are my servant too. God calls us to love and to serve each other. He says that a person that lays down his life for someone else shows the greatest love to that person." I then shared how Jesus was the greatest example of this in how he gave up his entire life to love and to serve others.

We continued the discussion while we worked. We talked about the joys that come when we serve, especially when that service is unsolicited or done quietly without asking for acknowledgment. We talked about how God says that everything that we do should be done as if we were working for God himself, no matter how mundane or meaningless it seemed.

That morning instead of a few minutes of math practice we enjoyed a priceless teaching moment that was infinitely more valuable.

Moms, we must not be so locked in our routines that we cannot be available to connect with our kids about the deeper, more important topics of life. These times to speak into our child's heart can't be scheduled or planned for, and yet they are one of the precious treasures of homeschooling.

"Schoolwork" Still Needs to Get Done

True, a flexible rhythm is great because life's interruptions are inevitable (and these challenges can be incredible learning experiences in themselves).

But thankfully a majority of our unplanned interruptions won't be huge life-altering events. They will be simple things like nursing a sick child, appointments that need to be scheduled during school hours, or quickly cleaning up the house before a last-minute play date.

But boy they can be frustrating. And if left unchecked they can easily add up and affect long-term goals we've made.

Here are some issues to think through if it feels like your school days are consistently being de-railed.

One-time occurrence or bigger issue? This is the first question I ask. If you notice that school always gets disrupted around 10:00 a.m., for example, ask yourself why. Is something happening within the family dynamics to produce this disruption? If a child becomes super squirmy at a specific time of the day (or during a specific subject), perhaps the rhythm isn't working and he may need a break or more kinesthetic activities at that time.

Or here's another example. You find that your normally content two-year-old becomes very grouchy after lunch on Thursday afternoons,

139

especially during the times when you're trying to help the older kids through their weekly science experiments. Each week, she clings to you and disrupts the teaching time with her attention- grabbing behavior. You think through the routine and realize that she is often left to play alone on Thursday mornings because those are the times when you teach the older girls key writing concepts. How can you re-arrange the family's week to give your younger daughter some one-on-one time on Thursdays (thereby encouraging better behavior and hopefully allowing the schoolwork to continue with fewer interruptions)?

Shorten or modify the lesson. If you notice a pattern of bad behavior, complaining and grouchiness around a particular subject, maybe take a closer look at what's happening. Is the learning approach (or the way the kids respond to the information, such as essay writing or oral narration) working? Maybe you're just trying to cover too much. Consider consolidating subjects or topics. Take inventory of the situation and determine if the lesson needs to be condensed or modified for the sake of the learning environment.

More than anything, trust the homeschooling process. This is not traditional schooling with its 8:00 a.m. to 2:30 p.m. time constraints! It is a blessing that we aren't required to define school as learning that occurs only within these hours! We're developing life-long learners.

Our goal is to give them a love of learning and to let them run with it—in whatever ways available on a given day.

Thankfully, we are given the freedom to let learning follow in a more realistic pattern and to insert creative solutions (if need be) to get that learning in.

Go mobile and get the work done on the road. This is where workbooks can be a life-saver. I personally don't like to over-use a workbook, but if we need to be out and about, it's a no-fuss easy way to get the work done.

If kids are older, they can do almost anything (short of a hands-on experiment or a messy art project) on the road. Thanks to internet-filtered laptops, phones and tablets, they can research projects, write essays—you name it.

Tablets and phones are also great for teaching younger kids on-the-go. There are tons of interactive readers and games for phonics, writing, geography, math—activities to match nearly every subject we study. It's a fun treat for the kids, and also a great way to review concepts.

Skip the lesson or subject for the day. Accept the fact that you may have a light homeschool day or week. This can't happen every week of course, but sometimes you just can't fit it all in, and that's alright. There's a natural ebb-and-flow to homeschooling: some weeks are heavy on the learning, and other weeks are light. On these lighter days, we have to trust the process that overall we're making strides toward our learning goals.

Say no to something else in order to get it done. If it's imperative that something's completed today or this week, consider saying no to another subject or commitment. The fact is that there's only so much time in a day, and if we say yes to one thing, sometimes we have to say no to something else. That's just reality.

If nothing else, read aloud to your kids. I can't tell you how many times we've sat in a doctor's examining room and read history or science books (either as read alouds or independent readers). Kids can learn so much when they simply read (or are read to)! In fact, there are entire curriculums like Five In A Row based around this concept.

If we've had a tough day and not much "school" has gotten done, the kids and I snuggle around a good book. It centers us as a family, grounds us back to our homeschool commitments, and (a nice benefit) it imparts an incredible amount of information. I find that reading aloud is like a soothing balm on those rough days.

Reading aloud can also be an effective strategy for those longer seasons when the rhythm is disrupted. My friend Katelin shares about a unique season in her homeschooling. When she was on bed rest while pregnant with her fourth child, she read extensively to her second grader, kindergartener and three year old. Because she spent her days in bed or on the couch, she termed it "couchschooling":

Whatever I could do from the couch, we did. Along with lots of children's literature, I read them The Burgess Animal Book and Christian Liberty Presses' history readers. My second grader read aloud to me and to the other children. They learned a lot that year, especially in science, because I took the time to field their questions and to have discussions. We would also play games like 'find me something that starts with the letter G' or for my three-year-old I'd say 'go find me three yellow things.' What else was I going to do? I was stuck on the couch or in bed!

I love this story because it reminds me that if life throws my schedule a major curveball, learning can still be accomplished by simply reading to my kids.

Action Plan:

1.   How do you react to the expected and unexpected interruptions to your routine?

2.   Do you see a pattern in any interruptions to your week? Do any of the above examples apply to what might be happening in your home?

CHAPTER 12:

Homeschooling with Joy and Freedom

Homeschooling has taught me to love disorder.

To love a messy stained countertop scattered with acrylic paint bottles, broken pieces of artist pastels, half-used watercolor pencils and partially completed canvases because that means that a child experimented with several different art mediums to express himself.

To see a desk crowded with stacks of paper, each filled with pictures, typed words and handwritten text: documented proof of a young mind that's gathering and sorting through knowledge.

To see eraser marks on paper because that means a new piece of information was learned and inserted to replace the previous information.

To see abandoned, half-created projects on my son's dresser because that means he created something, learned from it and knew when it was time to move on and try something else.

To hear my ten-year-old say, "Today I want to build a World War I bunker in the garage because I want to learn what it was like inside one," because that means he hasn't given up on learning and he wants to express his knowledge outside of "school hours."

It's taken me a long time to view these situations as evidence of real learning (and not plain messiness in my home).

Real Learning or Fact Recitation?

While we can set learning goals for each student, real learning (especially those lessons related to character training) can also be impromptu and often doesn't follow an anticipated pattern.

This doesn't mean that we should abandon our rhythms completely because real learning can't be organized and semi-structured.

Instead, it comes down to our view of what constitutes "real learning" and, subsequently, what parts of school we term as "successful" and "not successful." Do we look at half-created projects and consider the assignment a failure? Do we view requests for different ways to express knowledge as annoyances because they may require us to readjust the rhythm for the week?

Real learning is radically different from fact recitation. Real learning means that a person has fallen in love with knowledge, and has given themselves to a life of exploration and discovery. Fact recitation is the opposite: a lifeless, temporary gathering of meaningless information.

Of course we want our kids to have real learning over fact recitation! But we can't take a rigid hold on what "must happen in a day" so that real learning disguised as impromptu learning becomes a hindrance.

To explore this further, let's re-examine the "disorder" scenes presented in the beginning of the chapter.

Real Learning Muddled In the Chaos

First, let's consider the scene of the various art paints, pastels and pencils in disarray. Maybe a student started with one art medium, saw they didn't like it, and started over with a new canvas and a new medium (thus the partially completed canvas). Or maybe a young artist decided to use a combination of several mediums on one canvas. It could have been that there were several students here, each starting with a different art medium, but as the class time progressed, they inspired each other to try a combination of all three mediums. What was learned? Exploration, discovery and play through artistic expression. But did all of that experimentation fit in the time originally estimated for art? Maybe, maybe not.

Next, we see a desk crowded with stacks of paper, each filled with pictures, typed words and handwritten text. Information is being gathered and processed here. Sure, there's obviously been dedicated,

147

purposeful time to gather the information. But what if some of the gathering happened outside the confines of "class time"? Maybe the child read additional books on the topic in their free time, or that the solution to a difficult equation finally came to them at 2 a.m. This tells us that while setting routines for learning are essential, the "aha" moments—the ultimate goal of our learning—may come anytime.

What about the pencil eraser marks? Perhaps the child didn't understand the information within the time allowed. The eraser marks and crossed out words on a page reveal how complex and individual the learning process can be. You planned to spend tomorrow's class time delving into the next topic, but real learning may require that you plan a review time instead.

Or there may be times when a child abandons a project. Do we push them to complete it? Or do we allow them to try a different method for knowledge expression, even if pursuing a different avenue for expression will result in a change in that week's rhythm? Maybe they simply got bored or distracted and they need to be encouraged to finish. Or maybe the project is too hard, too complicated or not the right fit for their learning style and they need to try something else. There is no right answer here, but real learning requires that you take the time to consider the correct solution.

Lastly, there are those wonderful moments when a child embraces what he's been learning and wants to do additional study. When my ten-year-old talks about creating a life-size setup of something that we've been studying (such as the World War I bunker), I have two choices: to be annoyed by the potentially huge mess he may make; or to be excited for him because he's catching the vision for real learning. Either way, this additional study will probably be outside the time I'd loosely dedicated to that subject.

In these moments, we have to make the call as to where adherence to the rhythm is important; or whether we take a deep breath and allow this type of real learning to take over.

We have to be wise enough to see these opportunities, and, brave enough to adjust our original intentions for the day, if necessary, to let real learning happen.

The Fallacy of a "Complete" School Year

In late spring and early summer, a strange phenomenon happens for us homeschoolers. Others—especially those outside of the homeschooling community—begin asking us, "Are you done with school yet?" We get the opposite question in the fall: "When are you going back to school?"

It seems a strange concept to delineate "school" (especially something as natural as homeschooling) as having a start or stop date. Yet every year, in the late spring and early fall, we must field these questions.

Does anyone else see this definition of "today is a school day and tomorrow is not" as somewhat ridiculous?

Of course I understand the purpose behind the questions. Our society has been conditioned to the concept of a September to June school year, with a specific "break" from school in the summer months. The state must have some way of ensuring that kids are spending a certain percentage of their days in a year "doing school," and these days must be quantifiable on a calendar. This results in a nice, orderly system for determining when school is "in," and when school is "out."

Unfortunately, it can be ridiculous (and downright inaccurate) to label learning as happening only within these quadrants. This is especially true if you're trying to gift kids with the joy of lifelong learning because, by its very definition, learning doesn't have a "starting" and "stopping" point.

As we finish a school year, don't we all undergo a petering "in" and "out" of what would be called "traditional" study times?

During those last few weeks of May and in early June, I make goals and plans (and still generally live by the schedule) but I also begin a gradual transition of letting them all go.

We still complete our 175 required school days (I promise, State Board of Education!), but during this season those days are more relaxed. They are an unpredictable blend of, one day, lots of traditional "classroom" learning (as we finish up our projects and goals for the year) and, the next day, time with friends exploring outside (which I believe is just a different form of learning). Eventually this pattern becomes more play time and less traditional learning time. And then one day the kids say, "Mom, are we out of school yet?" and I say something like, "once we've finished this last part of our project, yes, we are done."

Does this mean that learning ends when our last day of school comes? Hardly! Truth be told, all homeschoolers probably do much, much more learning than our "required" school days. Think of all that summer holds: camping, trips to the beach or the lake, playing outside, hiking... the 19th century educator Charlotte Mason would call this "Nature Study" at its finest! And of course there's the summer reading programs and themed camps that many of our kids participate in.

The world outside our four walls is just begging us for discovery, especially this time of year. Like a woman with a beautiful new dress, the world in late spring and early summer is proudly on display and alive with color. The weather is warming, butterflies flutter through our backyards, flowers are in full bloom, lovely bird songs fill the air, and (thankfully) the days are longer to enjoy it all.

It's almost as if God himself is saying, "Come on out of your schoolbooks! Look at the magnificent, real beauty that I've created for this moment! Explore, learn and enjoy it all with me." Of course, being outside and enjoying creation is magnificent any time of year, but it seems like nature calls us the most loudly during spring and summer.

One of the homeschool bloggers I follow, Renee Tougas of Fun In My Backyard (fimby.tougas.net), lives in a rural part of Canada right next to the woods. In a post titled "Dropping It All," she describes how especially difficult it is for her family to stay inside during late spring (the time of year that most of us are ending our school year) and do what would be considered "traditional" schooling. As the world outside is awakened from its post-winter slushy state to a scene bursting with life and color, she and her children especially long to drop the schoolbooks and to go outside and to discover and embrace the beauty:

As our elementary school term ends, very unceremoniously, with the arrival of spring, I like to remind myself that a commitment to lifelong learning frees us from the need to start and end at certain times.

It also frees us up from the need to complete the workbook, complete the lessons, complete the term. Learning does not reach completion. Discreet projects and courses may be completed but the learning and application of math, writing, reading, history, etc... are not something you "finish".

During a season of school lessons (roughly fall and winter) I like having a plan to follow. I also like having this plan as a fall-back for those relaxed spring and summer months, on days or weeks when more direction and structure are needed.

I love making school plans but those are always subject to... pretty much everything else. Subject to birthday weeks, subject to spring, subject to my inspiration and motivation, subject to... real life.

And what I've learned through the years is that this is ok. It doesn't mean I am raising lazy, sloth children who will never apply themselves. It means I'm raising lifelong learners who know that learning is not limited to school lessons and textbooks.

I really love how she describes this delicate, slow fade of the schedule into the relaxing (yet still learning-filled) days of summer. It really is difficult to, as she describes it, "'wrap up' a homeschooling year nice and tidy, like a package with a bow."

I would add that it's also difficult (and unnecessary) to "finish" a book or particular curriculum by the end of a school year. Again, we all feel the "push" to finish that workbook or finishing our outlined objectives for the year. But if we succumb to this temptation, forced learning is almost always the result.

We needn't beat ourselves up for not "finishing" all that we'd outlined for the year. It's ludicrous that we should expect ourselves to perfectly outline in September what we will finish by June! And it's even more ridiculous to expect a pre-planned curriculum to accurately determine if we've "finished" for the year or not.

Instead, let's commit to working heartily toward our learning goals throughout the year, and then allow ourselves the freedom to say "nope, that's enough for now" at the end. You may spend two years going through a set of topics that was "supposed" to only take one year; or you may only cover half of the topics in a given curriculum. That's fine! The real question shouldn't be "Did we finish the curriculum?" but "Did quality learning take place during the year? Have the children progressed in their knowledge and skills in this area?"

There's no need to unnecessarily rush the learning. Remember, the information will always be there next year!

A Gentle Return to Formal Instruction

In addition, I would argue that the transition back into a school rhythm be more than (using Renee's "unwrapping a package" analogy from above) a mad dash to rip open a beautifully wrapped gift.

We just spent the majority of this book in preparation: reviewing what was working and not working; getting input from our kids on what they want to learn and how they want to learn it; investigating curriculum; calculating the arbitrary beginning and end of our school year; and formulating a weekly rhythm. What is the result of all this difficult work? The priceless, ornately wrapped gift of a potentially incredible homeschool year!

Why do we feel inclined to rush ourselves (and our children) into it? Why do we want to hastily rip off the wrapping paper, hurriedly shove the gift into a child's hands and demand that they play with it?

Perhaps we're excited to take these carefully chosen homeschool resources (the ones we've been poring over all summer!) finally out for a test drive on the open highway. Maybe we've greatly enjoyed our summer, but now we're longing for that comfort of a routine again, so we push, push, push our kids into a schedule. Or perhaps we like having the documented evidence to show those well-intentioned homeschooling naysayers that yes, the children are indeed receiving a fine education, thank you very much.

Instead, what if we returned to our traditional school year rhythm with as much flexibility as we let it go? Instead of pushing our kids off the diving board into the pool of learning (forcing them to quickly "sink or swim"), what if we took the shallow-end-route into the pool and allowed them to gradually acclimate to the water?

Remember that real learning is still happening (in various levels) when our kids are "off" school. When school begins again, we are simply changing the pace and returning to a more formal style of learning.

Going "back to school" doesn't have to be an abrupt, groan-inducing process, full of fights and tears. Think of it as a welcoming--a gentle slow nudge that encourages more structured study, but still leaves room for the untraditional forms of learning they enjoyed over summer break.

In the fall, as we begin the slow transition to a traditional school rhythm, the world outside will reflect this pattern. Deciduous trees slowly begin the process of returning to winter hibernation, and the temperature outside begins to have a decided chill. There will be cooler days as autumn draws nigh, interspersed with the occasional warm spell. The shift from summer to winter is a slow and gradual one, reminding us that our return to scheduled learning can be slow and gradual too.

Most days we can explore the new curriculum and test out the waters of a gentle routine, but there are those days when we can still enjoy the informal learning style of summer. Eventually, the routine becomes more comfortable, it becomes easier to stay inside and we find ourselves back in that scheduled "school" rhythm—happily plugging away at our educational goals for the year.

Welcome to the Learning Life

Learning is a journey that begins the moment we take our first breath and ends the moment we take our last and pass into eternity. Learning happens for a lifetime and it is a natural by-product of living.

During our children's first eighteen years of life, they have the opportunity to fall in love with knowledge. These are the moments that they begin their exploration of the world around us—taking in all the past, present and future realities.

These are the years when we are called to help our children establish strong morals and to develop character traits. Relationships and deep family bonds are developed during these times as well.

These high summits of homeschooling cannot be reached without long-term and yearly goal-setting, along with a commitment to purposeful living. This is life that, for the most part, is lived within the context of a purposeful-yet-flexible rhythm. This type of learning has a determined, persevering focus that make goals happen. It also has the wisdom to know when to drop those well-laid plans and to embrace the unexpected learning adventure of the moment.

It may not be a safe predictable life (and is often riddled with imperfection), but it is the learning life—the passionately lived life of those who plan to be flexible.

May you and your kids capture this beautiful vision for the learning life! Be encouraged that others around the world are catching the vision too, and growing in grace and wonder through the process. Our paths may each look a little different, but our vision is the same: to encourage our kids to be the well-rounded, self- motivated, strong leaders that our world so desperately needs.

Action Plan:

1.   How do you view "disorder" in your homeschool? Think through your everyday homeschool situations (like the ones detailed in the beginning of the chapter). Honestly assess how you view these situations. Do you see them as annoyances or disruptions to your "perfect" routine? Instead, is it possible that real learning is happening here?

2.   What does the transition "in" and "out" of a formal school schedule look like in your home? Consider how you and your children react to the change. Is it a forced, immediate schedule implementation or a gradual fade in-and-out of the rhythm?

APPENDIX

ASSESSMENT QUESTIONS:

What's Working (and What's Not) in Your Homeschool?

About the Curricula/Learning Style:

1.   Is real learning happening here? Do you see evidences of the child not only understanding the concepts but applying them in other school subjects and even in everyday conversation?

2.   Does your child have an excitement to learn this subject? Does it come alive for them?

3.   Do you battle with a child to complete a particular subject, and do you believe that the curricula may be partially to blame?

4.   Do the curricula allow for the type of learning that you've chosen for your homeschool (for example, interest-led learning, literature-based learning, etc)?

5.   Do the current curricula effectively teach the material for your students' grade level?

6.   Are the curricula easy-to-follow and to understand (for both you and the student)?

7.   Are accompanying resources easy to find?

8.   Are you comfortable with the amount of preparation time required for the curriculum?

9.   Are you content with the amount of hands-on teaching time required by the curriculum?

10.   Does the student enjoy the curriculum? Do you see his love of learning broadening because of the curriculum?

About the Student(s):

1.   What are his areas of weakness and areas of strength? What can you do to strengthen the weak areas?

2.   Does he have a specific subject that requires extra help, and will that require outside help (such as a tutor)?

3.   Are there core skills that you want him to learn by this time next year?

4.   Does he need to review past-learned concepts?

6.   Are there behavioral issues that need to be addressed?

7.   What is the student's general attitude toward school?

8.   Does he have adequate one-on-one teaching time with mom and independent learning time?

About the School Structure/Routine:

1.   Do the amount of school hours work for your students' needs and for the entire family schedule?

2.   Will there be an expected life change next year (for example, a new baby, a planned move, a part-time job for mom) that will require a change in the annual homeschool schedule or in the daily hours of schooling?

3.   Will a non-school aged child be changing to a new life stage that will require more attention (for example, a baby becoming a toddler)?

4.   Should you consider adding (or eliminating) out-of-the-home learning experiences, such as sports, clubs, or co-op teaching classes?

5.   Are there non-traditional school subjects that you'd like to include? Are there new household skills such as folding laundry and cleaning windows that students need to learn? How do you plan to incorporate learning activities such as

chores into the school day?

6.   Does anything need to change in your classroom workspace (or other area where you do school) to facilitate learning?

7.   Are there equipment, books, or software that need to be purchased to make learning easier?

8.   Do you need to implement organizational tools or systems to streamline the school day?

9.   What is the emotional tone of the classroom (Chaotic? Stressful? Creative? Frustrating? Relaxed?)? Is this in line with where you'd like it to be?

About the Teacher:

1.   Are there things about your teaching style that you'd like to change?

2.   Do you regularly exhibit the classroom behavior that you want your kids to have?

3.   Would you choose you as your teacher?

4.   If others also teach your child (such as in a co-op setting), are you content with the teaching methodology, or do you need to look for new outside teaching resources?

Made in the USA
Lexington, KY
31 May 2015